THE ULTIMATE INTENTION

"...I became a minister by appointment given to me for you from God, to accomplish **THE DIVINE INTENTION**, the secret hidden from the ages, and from the nations, but now made manifest to His saints by whom God has decided to publish amongst the heathen what is the wealth of that mystery of the rectification which Christ is to you--the hope of the rectification--which we proclaim; warning every man, and teaching every person in a perfect philosophy, so that we may present each one perfect in Christ; to which object I vigorously strive with His mighty energy working in me" (Col. 1:25-29, F. Fenton).

Published and Distributed

by

SURE FOUNDATION

Box 222

Mt. Vernon, Mo. U.S.A.

SURE FOUNDATION PUBLISHERS

*"...Behold I lay in Zion for a foundation
a stone, a tried stone, a precious corner
stone, a SURE FOUNDATION:..."*

First Edition
June, 1962

Second Edition
June, 1963

Third Edition
January, 1966

Fourth Edition
January, 1969

Fifth Edition
February, 1972

Copyright 1963

Introduction . . .

H. J. STANLEY

THROUGHOUT THE WORLD today there is the echo and re-echo of revolution. Surely this is evidence of the crisis hour in which we live. A NEW DAY is on the horizon. We are now in the night—a time of political, social, religious and philosophical shaking. Everything that can be shaken is being shaken. We can expect shaking to increase in tempo and momentum until only that which is unshakable remains. But we need not be alarmed, for God has determined to build anew on His SURE FOUNDATION—a foundation which cannot be shaken.

For this reason I believe it is time for a revolutionary note to be sounded in the Church. You will recognize in this Book such a note. Here is a challenge to reconsider some of the basic concepts which presently hold sway in evangelical circles.

Careful observation will disclose that the philosophical appeal of our current evangelistic endeavor is essentially selfish. The Church extends an offer that consists primarily of hope of gain and fear of loss for the individual—this suggests a "get" way of life! The fundamental of our invitation is for man to come to our church and get something for himself. Even our deeper life conferences are usually promoted on a man-centered level which suggests participants may obtain Christian victory and more profound blessings for their own heart satisfaction. It has become difficult for our generation to understand the real meaning of sacrifice, and the poured-out life is considered visionary. The rugged Pauline altar to which the great Apostle called men to come, suffer and die, has been replaced by the invitation to come to the altar and get over suffering. Our twentieth century altars are plush and comfortable. One approaches them to get and not to give.

We are past the point of revival; we have gone beyond the possibility of repair through reformation. Christianity must experience a vital revolution! The only solution to the problem of the Church today is a destruction of the philosophy that is ruining it and the introduction of another theme, a true goal, the real touchstone—one that is ultimate and final in every sense. Let me ask, is there a new frontier of truth in the Bible that must be discovered to furnish the supreme challenge to lives of old and young alike? Is there a hitherto unpenetrated spiritual barrier waiting for a breakthrough in our generation? Is there an unveiling of truth with power to bring lives to a dedication to God so as to fulfill His purpose in a measure and to a depth that no existing philosophy, either religious or political, at present is able to do? Let the reader of these pages decide for himself.

This book will unfold God's Word in a brand-new light. There are keys herein that can unlock the truth and bring divine transformation and power to the inner life. I say *can*, but I do not guarantee such experience. The great spiritual work in any life is God's to do, it is His sovereign prerogative.

To the readers, I recommend slow and careful study of the entire text. Evaluate and properly apply the meaning of words newly used in connection with divine relationships. Revolution is neither cheap nor simple. You are in for the "inner battle of your life." May God give His people grace to apprehend this great truth.

When Galilleo's discovery finally and authentically gave the earth a new center, it caused the greatest scientific revolution that had ever been known. The writings of centuries had to be adjusted in order for this truth to become the basis for mathematical and astronomical fact.

Thus it may be with much in our religious libraries when the facts of this book have gripped human lives.

INTRODUCTION TO SECOND EDITION

FOR MANY MONTHS, now, we have used *The Ultimate Intention* as a text in our midweek services at Lovers Lane Church. Among our dear people are those who are emerging into a purpose and philosophy of life that is wholly God-centered. Further, we have initiated what (to my knowledge) is almost an unprecedented thing: our church ministering to other pastors. God has given us the ministry of sharing this truth by sending the book to the clergy of our denomination. After months of receiving their grateful response, we are even more confirmed in our conviction that this is THE MESSAGE FOR OUR DAY. It simply must be shared with all who are honestly 'sick' of the status quo and are reaching out to for Himself.

Surely in keeping with the message of the book is the significant fact that SURE FOUNDATION is dedicated to making these books available below cost in quantities to all, that the truth might reach the entire Body of Christ. It is my prayer that each reader will not only be divinely *taught* but so utterly *caught* in the reading of these pages and the embracing of its truth that it will precipitate a chain-reaction reaching around the world and continuing UNTIL HE COMES!

—Pastor H. J. Stanley, Lovers Lane Church
Christian and Missionary Alliance, Akron, Ohio

Preface . . .

YOU WILL UNDERSTAND, if you have groaned as in travail and anguish to be delivered of a burden of prayer or message of truth, crying to the Lord for strength to bring forth, what I mean when I say this book has not been written; it has been born—born in the wee hours of the morning, and more often in the long hours of the night. The truths contained herein do not represent sudden conclusions or passing fancies, but they represent long months and years of prenatal growth until they have become overmastering and imperative. I appreciate your reading the preface for it will save you from wandering through many chapters, not clearly understanding the main thesis and burden of the author.

Without maligning or misreporting any man or any group of men, this small volume points to underlying principles which I believe to be the cause of the present spiritual climate, which supports a great deal of religious activity but little spiritual growth. It strives to open for the reader a broader view of God's purpose to be seen from a new viewpoint.

Our burden is this! The hour is too desperate for us to continue to play with surface issues. We must turn from our selfish playthings; we must cease our man-centered attempt to make religion serve us. It is imperative that we turn from recitation of tenets and defense of doctrine to a revelation of the basic issues and principles of the faith. We must choose deliberately to be nonconformists to the present world system, not because such an attitude coincides with the bent of our personality, but because we are *living by principle*.

It seems modern believers have imagined they can win men by agreeing with them. This is a farce that simply means they have won us. History demonstrates the exact opposite. Dr. A. W. Tozer points out, "The man who is going in a wrong direction will never be set right by the affable religionist who falls into step beside him and goes the same way. Someone must place himself across the path and insist that the straying man turn around and go the right direction."

NOT TRADITIONAL BUT SCRIPTURAL

It will be helpful from the very beginning, if the reader is made conscious that the message of this book does not follow the traditional, the modern evangelical, or fundamental approach. I am calling for a God-centered approach. If we observe the pattern which God has followed since the Reformation, we can see there has been a continuous recovery of Biblical and historic truths. Such restoration is imperative if the Church is to come to full maturity and bear fruit. Through Luther, God restored justification by faith; through Calvin, the importance of reasoning from God down to man; through Whitefield, Wesley and others, the emphasis of a holy, separated life; through Darby and others, glorious truths concerning the body of Christ and other Church truth. More recently, since 1900, the ministry of the Holy Spirit has been more generally recognized as an imperative need of the Church.

You may interpret this recovery of truth in your own way, but who can deny that God has used different men and movements—not to corner truth but to recover and herald truth to the upbuilding of the entire body of Christ. Every major awakening has centered in a major recovery of a truth necessary to mature and balance other aspects of truth.

I believe the hour has come when God is initiating another major recovery. This time it is not just a truth, but the restoration of something so imperative that it will give the ultimate perspective to all truth. Is it possible the Church is unable to fully appreciate or interpret the truth she has, simply because her perspective is wrong?

THE MAIN THEME

It is important that you immediately put on the right pair of glasses in order to see the path to ultimate truth. It is the objective of the first chapter to move the reader from his usual viewpoint to see things from God's viewpoint. Only then can ultimate issues be appreciated.

We make no appeal for man to come to God in order to be happy, to be blessed, or to be saved. Our approach is to urge men to wake up and become adjusted to the purpose for which they were created It is a call for man to realize *God's Ultimate Intention*. The primary theme of this book, then, is not man, his welfare, his needs, or his salvation.

The primary theme purposes to reveal *who God chiefly is* so we can understand what He primarily desires and ultimately intends *for Himself* and for His universe. The first concern is not to turn our attention to man's problems, but rather to turn our eyes to God Himself. The primary emphasis is not the awful emergency which sin has caused, but the purpose of One who will most surely consummate His intention according to schedule. The primary motive of our writing is to bring men to *really* see HIM who is worthy of all honor, glory and satisfaction. Once we see Him and His purpose, we shall see all other things in their true light and perspective.

MAN-CENTERED or GOD-CENTERED

Believers may not often realize it, but even as believers we are either centered in man, or centered in God. There is no alternative. Either God is the center of our universe and we have become rightly adjusted to Him, or we have made ourselves the center and are attempting to make all else orbit around us and for us. When the truth dawns, we are amazed to discover how the snare of making all things to revolve around man has become the bane of most of our preaching and teaching. This is true even of the area of teaching which is considered to be of the deeper life emphasis. As long as men are victims of this wrong philosophy and approach to truth, they cannot avoid reckoning from a self-center. When the center is wrong, then everything in our reckoning is wrong. It is my prayer that in these pages the reader will discover the lost coin of truth and be prepared to take what may seem like drastic measures in accepting a *new center*, where the whole conception of Christian life is changed from man-consciousness to God-consciousness; from man as the center to God as the center from which all truth is seen.

A SHOCK TREATMENT

Electric shock treatments are used in treating mental patients in order to break up old patterns of thought and prepare the way for new ones. The moral and spiritual crisis leading to surrender is a similar experience. It breaks up the old patterns of self-centeredness and shifts to a new center—GOD. Various shocks are often necessary to blast us from the pseudo-centers we have established, before the Holy Spirit can draw us to the ultimate center. Until we place ourselves in God's hands for His treatment, we may be centered in an experience, a group, an emphasis of truth, a spiritual person, our work, or a religious cause. All of these are marginal. As false centers, they become false viewpoints, and lead to faulty understanding of truth. It often takes quite a shock to cause us to organize life around a new center. A certain measure of healing is to be found in any center of life outside oneself, but there is no ultimate healing until we find the *ultimate center*.

You are anticipating a shock! May the Holy Spirit place His finger on the false center around which your life revolves and make you free! We earnestly pray this vital truth might lay hold of lives so as to initiate repercussions to ignite spiritual revelation around the world. This, no doubt, seems like strong language, but we are sure that until one has grasped the value and significance of *this viewpoint*, he cannot properly evaluate the necessity for its recovery by the Church in this hour.

I am convinced of the importance of this message as I have observed the impact and revolutionary effect it has produced in pastors and laymen who have been gripped by it. These lives speak louder than any appraisal I might attempt.

THE NEUROSIS OF OUR TIMES

There is a sense in which I understand how Jeremiah must have felt when he was commissioned to "root out, to pull down, to destroy and to throw down" (four negatives) before he could begin to "build and plant" (the positives). Before positive restoration can proceed, false foundations must be exposed and destroyed. In these desperate days of spiritual lethargy and confusion, we must with a prophetic voice call a halt to all this beating of the air and fumbling around with surface issues. The present message of the Church simply does not awaken men or uncover the deepest need. There is deep-seated disillusionment amid the frenzied activity of the Church; there is a strange emptiness.

One well-known diagnostician writes: "About a third of my cases are suffering from no clinically definable neurosis, but from the sense-lessness and emptiness of our lives. This can well be defined as the central neurosis of our times."

The human personality simply cannot survive in an empty, meaningless universe. It is alarming to see not only those outside, but even some inside the church who are going to pieces. Men are tired of being pushed into an empty routine labeled "Christian activity." There is something within every man which soon revolts against *doing*, so he will be rewarded with crowns. No matter how perverted · and self-centered he is, if there is a spark of godly desire, man will eventually react negatively to this. Because the moral tissue within has not been completely deadened, he will come to hate his own selfishness. He yearns for deliverance from the emptiness of serving self in a religious system which says, "Find happiness and satisfaction in serving the Lord."

ATTITUDE IS IMPORTANT

In this modern day of religion, education, science and philosophy, many have insisted there is no ultimate touchstone for reckoning; all is bound by the law of change; all is relative. Not only is there a general rejection of the idea of ultimate basis for reckoning, but there is a downright antagonism to *anything* absolute or ultimate in a final sense. If you have unwittingly imbibed this spirit, which has invaded even evangelical circles, we trust you will purpose in your heart to reserve judgment of the material presented here until the book has been read and evaluated as a whole.

We approach the vast and magnificent theme of GOD'S INTENTION with humility, and pray that you will join in the study with the same spirit. For who among mortal men could ever adequately deal with *God's Ultimate Intention?* Yet, we believe He has designed for us to understand the ultimate principles upon which are based the unfolding of His purpose throughout the ages. We are gently restrained by the Holy Spirit from attempts to probe or press beyond that which He has revealed in His Word, or to proceed on the false assumption that everything in heaven or earth can be explained. Let this be our rule, "The meek will He guide in judgment (critical evaluation): and the meek will He teach His way" (Ps. 25:9). Be assured of His promise; He will guide!

We must also observe the careful balance between God's part and our part in the pursuit of truth. All the while we are expectantly waiting for His sharing of truth, we must be learning to think. "Human thought has its limitations, but where there is no thinking there is not likely to be any large deposit of truth in the mind. Evangelicals at the moment appear to be divided into two camps: those who trust the human intellect to the point of sheer rationalism, and those who are shy of everything intellectual and are convinced that thinking is a waste of the Christian's time." (A. W. Tozer).

CAUTIOUS, BUT CURIOUS

Because there are so many things to read these days, we are concerned that God's children develop the faculty of spiritual discernment so as to avoid error. There are so many areas of Christian thought and life where likenesses and differences are so difficult to distinguish that we avoid the snare only as God helps us to develop both a sharp eye and a proper yardstick for measuring facts.

In our travel we observe scores who are being deceived by error, misplaced emphasis, or a combination of both. This results from weakness in some aspect of the spiritual walk. But while it is right to be cautious, yet we must remain curious. God has made us to wonder. He has implanted this faculty which, when properly functioning, is ever calling out for the unfolding of truth. Spiritual hunger, then, is a genuine curiosity.

It is my settled conviction that once the reader has grasped the thesis of this book, he will find the answer to the deepest gnawing of his heart for ultimate answers. We know that in the physical realm a constitutional deficiency, or a lack in the diet, causes a person to become susceptible to the many maladies floating about. So it is in the spiritual realm. This may be manifest in individual believers or in an assembly. Because the hunger of the heart has not been satisfied, there is a constitutional weakness. This is manifest in the daily lives of the underfed flock and in their susceptibility to spiritual maladies and various kinds of wrong emphasis.

The basic lack is a central, unifying, defensive position—an *ultimate viewpoint* from which believers can properly understand the purpose, value and significance of all of life. Of course, the author believes such a touchstone for truth exists, but has been lost by the Church, otherwise such a book as this would be unnecessary.

MODERN COUNTERFEITS

Where there is no ultimate viewpoint and men relate everything to themselves and measure truth with a human yardstick, there is inevitable fragmentation and distortion of truth. Cults are evidence of this phenomenon. You will find that off-color religious groups put much emphasis on the ultimate issues of life. But because they have invaded these areas, must we continue to neglect them? God forbid! The alarming growth of false cults, especially in America, is a resounding indictment on the evangelical church. It is time to recognize that only whole truth—unbroken and undistorted—will meet the need of the whole man. While we should have been teaching people to think in order that their hunger for truth might be satisfied, we have instead prescribed what is to be received as truth. Because they have treated truth as though it were contained in rather small, easy to be grasped packages, men have inferred it could be received one package at a time, opened, and used as it best suits their needs.

Some minds sense that truth is a vast ocean, and when they do not find adequate answers in the packages handed them in the average church, they seek elsewhere. Because they have not been given an ultimate goal, nor the proper instruments for navigation on so wide an ocean, they flounder into some treacherous lagoon where they drift without chart or compass. If emphasis on proper thinking were given place in the church, such cults as Christian Science, Unity, Christ Unity Science, Religious Science, New Thought, and the rest would never have gained foothold. Those mentioned know no triune God, no incarnate Word, no vicarious sacrifice and no risen Saviour. But they have an appeal to the natural minds of men who have not found adequate answers in the average church.

Surely this is the hour of judgment. Our country is being engulfed by a deluge of Eastern philosophy and esoteric teaching which has great appeal to those who have become sickened by the gross materialism of the West. Such illicit doctrines always seem to carry more appeal for the lustful, natural mind. Because they "loved not the truth" He sent "strong delusion" that they might believe a lie. But we must not answer this invasion of Satan with evasion. The human heart longs to know the ultimate of God.

Survey the teachings of the cults and you will discover that they are always attempts to get at ultimate issues; they are intent on bringing adherents to a new way of thinking, a new philosophy of life. They offer "peace of mind" or "healing" to those who will "sit where they sit, so as to see as they see." They know one is not converted to the fundamental issue around which they center until his thinking has been bent to their point of view. This reveals the weakness of too many church groups. Adherents are not expected to probe beneath the surface of truth dealt out in packages—simple as a do-it-yourself kit or a box of ready-mix. There is no appeal for a basic change in philosophy, nor is there a message which ultimately rectifies false views and produces a God-centered philosophy of life.

Knowing this to be our deepest need, we can see why Paul in writing to the Corinthians unveils God's primary objective in sending His Son: "Christ Jesus brought a philosophy from God to us, as well as righteousness, and purity and redemption" (1 Cor. 1:30, Ferrar Fenton). By this divine philosophy, man's greatest questions and problems are answered, and through obedience to it, he is utterly rectified to God. Here we should point out that the word "philosophy" means love of wisdom and has to do with the study and knowledge of the principles that cause and explain facts and events. We urge, therefore, that you not fear the term, but rather learn to distinguish between the philosophy of men and that divine philosophy which is given in God's Son.

A FINAL CONCERN

If you, like many, have been accustomed to using the microscopic method of Bible study, which scrutinizes every detail and phrase in order to understand the will and purpose of God, may God help you to shift gears! The method of this book is telescopic instead of microscopic. We shall be concerned with presenting a panoramic sweep of the ultimate truths of God's Word. It is my conviction that we have too long been involved with a method which centers attention on immediate details without reference first to the larger scope of God's purpose. We have been majoring in minors. We have been more alive to the marginal than the central. We have become so accustomed to speaking in comparatives that we are almost afraid of superlatives. Let us make the necessary mental adjustments, move to the God-centered viewpoint, and take an entirely fresh look at the old, old truths of God's Word.

DEDICATION

To the many who have come to know and appreciate these Ultimate Truths as they have been shared around the world — whose lives have thereby become fruitful UNTO HIM . . . .

and

. . . to those who even now in the reading of these pages may join in His ULTIMATE DEDICATION as we have portrayed it in the closing chapter — this book is prayerfully dedicated.

Contents . . .

It is Imperative. . . .

. . . THAT WE RECOGNIZE the deepest gnawing within the human breast is for adequate answers to the purpose and meaning of life. Man can only be a saint or a sinner by choice, but he is first a philosopher by nature. "There is no attribute of man's personality more evident and universally recognized among men than this sense of purpose and of divine destiny " (C. A. Jones).

Just as every mother is disappointed if her child never asks the question *why*, so God must be concerned when men attempt to stifle the built-in philosophical urge which He has put within every breast. Take the philosopher out of man and he ceases to be the man God created. Destroy his sense of destiny and purpose and he soon becomes nothing more than a beast.

Therefore, it is imperative that we direct every believer to develop a truly God-centered philosophy of life—this means we must see all things as properly related to God and His ultimate intention. Alas, not only the worldling, but even the believer attempts to interpret all things as they primarily relate to himself. And then he is amazed when he cannot avoid the paradoxes which seem to nullify his attempt to see life steadily and see it whole.

It was the intention of our Father-God that all men might find the answers to life's deepest enigmas. It was because of this imperative need in man that "Jesus Christ brought a philosophy from God to us, as well as righteousness, and purity and redemption" (Ferrar Fenton's Translation 1 Cor. 1:30). Why did He do this? So that He might become the answer to man's greatest questions and problems, and fully rectify him to fulfill the *DIVINE INTENTION*.

As the Psalmist suggests (Ps. 103:7), most people only observe the acts of God but never, like Moses, come to know the ways of God. Consequently there is much on the surface that seems confusing. This is because we have not discovered the ways in which the parts are integrated into the whole. Mark Fakkema suggests:

Underneath apparent antagonisms, philosophy holds that there is an inner coherence, making for a basic unity and integration of all things. We can say that philosophy is the endeavor to unite things in a universe of thought making for a unified rationale. Philosophy, in surveying the totality of life, seeks to integrate in one's thinking all things into a single pattern of thought. Christian philosophy is the romance of seeing all things as one whole with God as ULTIMATE.

Too often there has been an overemphasis on various aspects of truth, each of which plays its own important part. Some truths have almost neutralized their influence because we have ignored the greater whole of which they form a part.

It is also true that each one of us is constantly growing. That is, as our minds are reaching out for more truth—for some new facet of reality—which must be temporarily spotlighted. This throws the matrix from which the truth emerged back into the shadows. At this point we must be very careful. It will be our purpose throughout the sections of this book to spotlight various phases, such as:the Father from whence all purposes begin, the purpose of creation, the destiny of man, the result of the Fall, the divine intention in the Cross, the purpose for Christ's incarnation, the reason for suffering, etc. But always we shall insist that the reader learn to see these aspects as related to the *WHOLE* — to see the matrix out of which each is born.

The following quotation from *The Diagnosis of Man* by Kenneth Walker, illustrates how longstanding our difficulty is, and our need for fresh vision to see life steadily and see it whole:

The Disagreement as to the Description and Shape of the Elephant :

The elephant was in a dark house: some Hindus had brought it for exhibition. In order to see it, many people were going, every one, into that darkness. As.seeing it with the eye was impossible, each was feeling it in the dark with the palm of his hand.

The hand of one fell on its trunk: he said, 'This creature is like a water-pipe.' The hand of another touched its ear: to him it appeared like a fan. Since another handled its leg, he said, 'I found the elephant shape to be like a pillar.' Another laid his hand on the back: he said, 'Truly this elephant was like a throne.'

Similarly, when anyone heard a description of the elephant, he understood it only in respect to the part he had touched.

In commenting upon this illustration A. Graham Ikin suggests: "All our cross-sections of reality are like this. They are real points of contact with the whole that unites them. It is fruitless to waste time standing out for any particular finite viewpoint as exclusive or total, or quarreling with those who from another human viewpoint have seen another aspect. We need to pool our partial insights, not ignoring others, nor depreciating or apologizing for our own, but accepting each as valid within its own sphere and making its own contribution to the integrated complexity of the whole."

This is good advice, but it is still merely man attempting to understand the significance of the whole from his own standpoint. And this has too long been the source of our trouble.

If you miss the eternal outlook you will miss the thesis of this book and the primary intention of the author. It is our purpose to lift the reader out of *time* into the eternal so that he will be able to share God's point of view. Only as one begins in God, to view *His Ultimate Intention*, can he have a proper outlook, awareness or expectancy.

We can best illustrate the relation of the eternal One to us in time by thinking of the relation of a reader to the events in a story book. While the reader lives in a realm altogether different from the time sequence of the book, yet he projects himself into page after page of the story. As pages are turned, certain incidents go into the past, others come into the present, and yet others remain in the future. No matter to what page he turns, the events are all present, and actually happening for him at the moment he reads.

This is the way God views history. As someone has said, "To Him our lives with their past and future are all present; our yesterdays as well as our tomorrows are all NOW to Him."

Throughout the coming chapters we shall accept God's invitation to live in the eternal and to see how all things in time are related to Him. We shall consider the whole progressive unfolding of God's ultimate intention. This is *His-story*, too long viewed as though it were man's story.

As we look out from the *eternal*, we will discern three major faults in viewing history from other points of view. While these errors may

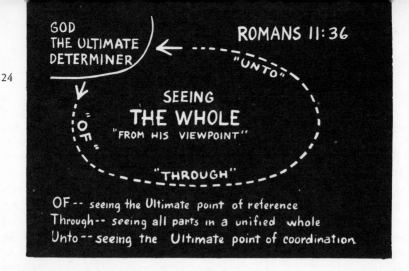

GOD
THE ULTIMATE
DETERMINER

ROMANS 11:36

"UNTO"

SEEING
THE WHOLE
"FROM HIS VIEWPOINT"

"THROUGH"

OF -- seeing the Ultimate point of reference
Through-- seeing all parts in a unified whole
Unto-- seeing the Ultimate point of coordination

not be fully apprehended at the beginning, they will become clearer and more meaningful as we move along.

First, because we usually start from the wrong point, we develop a *false point of reference.*

Second, because we take the part as though it were the whole, we develop a *fatal near-sightedness.*

Third, because we start wrong, our procedures become wrong, and therefore our progress is off-course. We have *no proper point of coordination.*

Since the Fall, blinded man has ever continued to make himself central. From his point of view, even in the religious realm, concepts and resulting methods become twisted until it often seems the church is presenting a God whose entire working is for man—his benefit, welfare, blessing and bliss.

Some will admit they frankly feel this is the true work of the church. Who else is important? What else should we preach? Who else but man is important to God? Does not God Himself expend all His energies and purposes *for man?*

Yes, until man has had a major rectification he will, even as a believer, be the very center of his very small universe—seeking to make all things serve himself.

Perhaps you have wondered why it has been difficult for the Church, through the centuries, to blossom into the full maturity which God intended—the Church which Paul describes in Ephesians 4. This is not impossible! It is God's purpose for His people. The hour is now upon us when He is doing a very special thing. It should be no cause for surprise, if the truth He is now unveiling causes a violent reaction. His Body must grow to maturity. The old wineskins cannot possibly contain what God is now preparing and doing.

The secret of realizing God's ultimate intention is to be found in

the correction of vision, i.e. *establishing a true point of reference,
seeing the whole of God's intention, discovering the lost point of coordination.*

We shall see how our ultimate starting point in God determines all
basic concepts. Once the significance of this becomes fully apparent,
it will also be evident to multitudes of leaders in the religious world
that a very real upheaval and revolution in basic concepts is indicated.
Such an upheaval was seen when the Apostle Paul interpreted the
significance of God's new order, the Church, as distinguished from the
Judaistic system. We can be sure when today His Church rises to
fulfill her true calling, something equally revolutionary will be seen.

To understand the adjustment necessary to bring our vision into
focus from God's point of view, let us look at modern Christendom.
While many leaders mark with concern the drift in evangelical circles,
efforts to turn the tide usually miss the heart of the problem. Although
most will readily agree that it is proper to *begin with God*, in practice
they actually begin with man and make him the center. Consider three
segments of Christendom and their differing burdens:

The *Liberal* sees the desperate needs of mankind and would emphasize the social work that needs to be done *by man*.

The *Fundamentalist,* while recognizing social needs, knows the
emphasis must first be placed on understanding that which God has
done *for man*.

A third segment, often called the *holiness groups,* insists that all
this is too shallow and they would place emphasis rather on the work
which God must do *in man*.

While each segment carries forward in terms of its emphasis, and the
battle may sometimes rage between them, the real issue is altogether
missed. It is *man* they are primarily occupied with. There is another
side of the coin which has too long been ignored. It is this side we
must consider first if all things are to be properly related to God as
the Center. When the work of the church is man-centered — starting
with man, centered in his needs, conscious of his welfare, and seeking
his blessing—we have the wrong center of gravity. However much God
may have done for man and in him, man is still out of proper orbit until
his deepest and most basic need has been met. This greatest of all
man's needs is an *ultimate rectification* from himself as the center
unto God as the center. The Scripture emphasizes this imperative need
through Paul's writing: "We speak, instead, a divine philosophy . . .
for our rectification" (F. Fenton 1 Cor. 2:7).

As long then as believers live in time and are centered in man's interest, our preaching, teaching and service will be

... man-centered instead of God centered.

... redemptive and kingdom conscious instead of eternal   purpose conscious.

... heaven and glory conscious (for man) instead of for the ultimate satisfaction, glory and honor of God.

God's call to repentance was a call to *metanoia*, as the Greek stresses. This means a turning from sin, from the old life and its pursuits, but even more it means a call to an utter change of mind, a new way of looking at things. Thus, true repentance must never stop short of ultimate rectification: living wholly for all that God ultimately intends.

Finally, it is imperative for us to see how all that the eternal Father has desired, purposed and intended *for Himself* becomes the key for understanding what He ultimately intends (1) for His lovely Son, (2) for man, (3) in the Cross, (4) during this age, and (5) in the ages to come. Surely all our living will come short of His ultimate intention until we come to the fuller meaning of these three ultimate themes: *revelation, rectification* and *realization.*

On the blackboard we picture these three ultimate themes to be pursued throughout our study:

The REVELATION of the FATHER — who He chiefly is, what He desires, purposes and intends, (our point of reference);

The RECTIFICATION of all things to *God's ultimate intention* (considering the whole of God's purpose rather than a part);

The REALIZATION of all that God originally purposed (finding our point of coordination in Him).

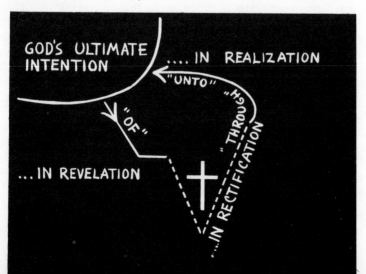

Paul sums up the whole scope of our study in short terms when he says: "For of Him, and through Him, and to Him, are all things: to whom be glory for ever. Amen" (Rom. 11:36).

(a) All things are *of* God. This implies something more than *from* God. As an image in the mirror is of its original, so all things can be said to be *of* God.

(b) All things are *through* God. All things are sustained constantly by the breath of His might. In Him we live and move and continually have our very being.

(c) All things are *unto* God. All things find their ultimate intention and purpose in God.

So our course is indicated by the three prepositions: *of, through* and *unto*. Let us see how God is our starting point. Then we shall see how all things find their proper relatedness and true meaning as they fulfill HIS ULTIMATE INTENTION.

AS WE discover what it means to live in His eternal outlook, and view the parts as they are related to the whole, we shall see how imperative it is to have . . .

The Proper Starting Point

HOW SHALL WE PICTURE IT: The fact that most often our conceptions are wrong because we start at the wrong place? Too often human history has been interpreted from the Fall. If this is the starting point ("D" on the blackboard) it is natural that all history would have a redemptive coloring. God's purpose is then seen in the light of man's need for redemption. Of course the need for redemption must not be minimized, but neither should it become the overshadowing truth.

It is often made to seem that man appeared on the stage of time just so he could be saved. Thus it seems man becomes important in God's purpose *only in his fall.* Therefore, God's chief work is seen as redemptive.

We cringe at the thought, and deep within we are sure there must have been some "better purpose," yet if we start with man and his fall we seem to be carried along in a conception which makes man and his restoration to be central. Because our controlling conception was born from the wrong starting point—man and his fall—we can but end with man and his restoration. But there are others, sensing this danger, who have started with God's commission to Adam, "Be fruitful and multiply and fill the earth, and subdue it" (Gen. 1:28). From this starting point ("C" on the blackboard) all history is interpreted with

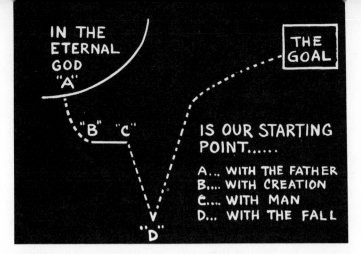

a governmental or kingdom purpose. Since man was created to rule, he sees everything as colored by this conception. The kingdom becomes the central theme.

Then there are those who have realized the need for starting with God instead of with man. So they have started where God starts in Genesis 1:1— with God as Creator. From this starting point (point "B") the resulting scheme and purpose of God has an architectural or sovereign coloring. But while allowing for a God-centered approach, this doesn't fully answer the purpose in His creation nor describe His sovereignty.

We wonder if there is not a more ultimate starting point which will solve the enigma of life and purpose? Suddenly we recognize why the Apostle Paul always started back in the heart of the eternal Father before the foundation of the world. Paul always started with God's vital (or self-sharing) Fatherhood. (See point "A" on blackboard). It was not with the Father's varied activities, nor with His wondrous attributes that Paul started; it was with the Person, who He chiefly is: THE FATHER. Thus *God's vital Fatherhood* is seen to be the controlling and ultimate factor which determines all His activities.

From this (ultimate) starting point, looking out from His Paternal eyes, we see all that the Father purposed as His ultimate intention or *eternal goal.* Everything takes on full meaning when it has a *paternal coloring.* We understand *why* He has done all He has. New light breaks on the future. What would a Father desire, purpose and ultimately intend?

The next lesson will consider this eternal outlook from the heart of the Father. But before turning to a more detailed consideration of God's original purpose, let us make sure we understand how imperative it is to have an ultimate starting point.

If you will open almost any present-day religious book or periodical, you will discover the degree to which modern Christendom is centered in man. Furthermore, God's primary purpose is set forth as redemptive. The overshadowing theme of religious writing is man's fall, his various needs and God's provision for meeting them. In this way God is always related to man's benefit, blessing and future. Man becomes central; but is this God's intention?

This evidence of a man-centered approach and message indicates the desperate cancer which is eating at the heart of Christendom. It is the result of a warped concept developed by blinded man who has, ever since the Fall, made all to center around and for himself.

To discover the truth of this broad indictment against modern Christendom, the reader is invited to consider not only how God is *central* in the universe, but how His vital Fatherhood is the controlling factor which determines His plan, purpose and intention.

What did the Father intend, in the eternal past, *had sin never entered the world?* The line on the blackboard was to have gone straight, without a downward break. It has been this writer's conviction for many years that Paul unveils in the Ephesian letter that which had always been in the mind of the Father. A moral Father could not do otherwise than allow moral agency to His created children. Thus the entrance of sin was not in any way necessary, nor was it designed, nor has it altered God's ultimate intention or purpose. The crisis arose because of man's action outside God's purpose. Therefore the line dropped to "D" from which it must be brought up again. This is what we see as we observe man's failure. Yet God's ultimate intention has never changed.

FROM ETERNITY THE PATERNAL PURPOSE IN THE SON

How shall we make it clear that there is an eternal purpose hidden in the Father which has never been involved in time? This is clearly set forth by Paul in Ephesians 1:4, "According as He hath chosen us in Him before the foundation of the world. . . ." Here is something that moves on the eternal level—not at all affected by sin or by time. It is something the Father has already seen in consummation. Furthermore we must see how the eternal Son is related to this eternal purpose of the Father. We have been so prone to relate Christ to the redemptive activity that we have hardly appreciated how He is related to eternity and the Father's purpose.

Perhaps we can move the eternal Christ into a proper frame of reference by asking; if man had never sinned, would all things have been summed up in Christ? (Eph. 1:10). If man had never sinned was it

God's plan for all to be *"in Christ?"* If man had never sinned would Christ have been incarnated into the human family? It seems evident from Paul's writing in Ephesians as he moves on the eternal level that the Father intended for His Son to be a means of accomplishment, not because sin entered, but even if sin had never entered. Consider these statements:

vs 3 "... blessed us ... in Christ"

vs 4 "... chosen us IN HIM before the foundation ... "

vs 5 "... predestined unto adoption ... BY JESUS CHRIST ... "

vs 6 "... accepted IN THE BELOVED ... "

vs 10 "... gathered together all things ... IN CHRIST ... "

We must cease interpreting God's purpose and plan in the light of the Fall. This which we see in Ephesians is what the Father intended to realize in His Son and it has never been affected by sin, the fall, or time.

It was this purpose which had previously been a mystery, that the Apostle Paul was now unveiling: The Father intended for HIS SON to have a Body to express His life—HIMSELF—in the world now, and before all creation in the ages to come.

We can quickly see how this ultimate intention for THE SON and His Body springs out of God's paternal nature and desire. We can also understand how the Father "marked out for Himself" a vast family who would share His life, nature, spirit, vision, purpose and dedication. We can further see how this *family purpose* was to be accomplished both through and for His eternal Son.

We have said that God's line of purpose was to have gone upward, without a break. But because man must be allowed opportunity to choose cooperation in God's purpose, we see how man also could choose to go his own way. As a result God's plan in time necessitated the incorporation of the redemptive plan. But He never intended that this redemptive phase was to overshadow the *original eternal purpose.* As we have said, in temporarily "spotlighting redemption" we have too often thrown the matrix out of which it emerged back into the shadows, until it has almost been overlooked.

I like the way Watchman Nee puts it:

We only see history back to the Fall. God sees it from the beginning. There was something in God's mind *before* the Fall, and in the ages to come that thing is to be fully realized. God knew all about sin and redemption; yet in His great purpose for the Church set forth in Genesis 2 there is no view of sin. It is as though (to speak in finite terms) He leaps in thought right over the whole story of redemption and sees the Church in future eternity, having a ministry and a (future) history which is altogether apart from sin and wholly of God. It is the Body of Christ in glory, expressing nothing of fallen man but only that which is the image of the glorified Son of man. *This* is the Church that has satisfied God's heart and has attained dominion.

As we move away from our earth-bound viewpoint to the heavenly vantage point of eternity, we shall see the wonders of His eternal purpose encompassing, but far exceeding, the wonders of redemption. For the Father from eternity had a wonderful purpose for Himself which of course included man. Redemption is not the end, but only a recovery program. It is but a parenthesis incorporated into the *main theme*.

This is the reason for insistence on starting in the Father-heart with His desire, purpose and intention. By doing this we shall see Christ from a very different point of view. He is not related primarily to man's need, but to the Father's ultimate intention. Since God's plans and purposes are not determined by man's need, let us henceforth see how all things take on new meaning and purpose when they are properly related to Him for His honor, glory, pleasure and satisfaction.

LOOKING OUT from His eternal viewpoint our near-sightedness is gone. We begin to appreciate how all that God does is perfectly integrated into His whole inten-tion. Instead of having only a collection of facts con-cerning the totality of things, we see all in its proper frame of reference. We can see new meaning and eternal purpose in all things as they are related to this . . .

One Ultimate Theme

HOW GREAT A DAY when we have moved beyond the separate strands to see the firmly woven cord of the Father's eternal purpose and ultimate intention. Too long have we each, like the blind men of Hindustan, interpreted life from a partial conception. In the previous chapter we have realized how God's vital Fatherhood is the ultimate starting point by which we can measure everything in its true di-mension.

Without knowing life's ultimate meaning, men have too long been forced to label things *a mystery*. They have spoken of the mystery of His will, the mystery of creation, the mystery of suffering, the mystery of His ultimate intention. But it is high time to recognize that He *has* given a "light that shines in the darkness." The darkness cannot forever eclipse the Father's intention in mystery, because now the light of the Eternal Father is breaking through to unveil His heart, desire, purpose and intention in order that His children might move into the fuller dimensions of life.

Perhaps the most common error of which we have all been guilty is confusing the means and methods with the end. By making man the central benefactor of God's purpose, it has seemed that his conformity to the image of Christ was the end—yet it is only a means to a greater end. Others have made salvation or entrance into heaven to be the end. Others have assumed that completing His glorious and spotless Church was the end, or that bringing all things to the universal reign of the kingdom was the end, but alas, these are only important means by which God will achieve His greater end. As long as we come short of understanding *God's ultimate intention*, we shall be centered in the means and methods and never fully comprehend the true dimensions and meaning of life and the purpose hidden in the Father-heart.

On the blackboard we have pictured strands which comprise the "cord of eternity." This cord is woven with many of the means and methods by which the Father will realize His eternal purpose. We can only comprehend the part each fills as we unfold the various strands and see their related importance in the light of God's overall plan. In the previous lesson we have observed the *Paternal theme* which runs throughout the eternal purpose. Many marvel that they have missed it so long. For Paul has answered in one sentence: (Eph. 1:3-4) most of the questions we might ask about the Father and this vast family He has marked out for Himself, which is now being realized through His only begotten Son:

WHO . . . . . "He" (God, the Father) vs. 3

WHAT . . . . "chose us" (picked us out as sons for His family).
　　　　　　　vs. 4

HOW . . . . . "In Him" (Christ—the eternal Son involved in all
　　　　　　　aspects). vs. 3, 4, 5, 6, 7. 10.

WHEN . . . . "before the foundation of the world . . ." vs. 4

WHY . . . . . "for Himself," as His own (for His pleasure, glory
　　　　　　　and satisfaction).

WHERE . . . that we should be "before Him" ("in His immediate
　　　　　　　presence." K. Wuest) vs. 4

EACH STRAND ONLY A PART

Thus we have Paul's birdseye view of what was in the mind and heart of the Father before He started any of the vast activity by which this eternal family would be realized.

To attempt to understand the reason for creation when we start with God as a Creator leaves us with an enigma. It is only when we start

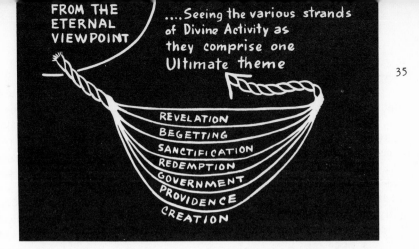

FROM THE ETERNAL VIEWPOINT ....Seeing the various strands of Divine Activity as they comprise one Ultimate theme

REVELATION
BEGETTING
SANCTIFICATION
REDEMPTION
GOVERNMENT
PROVIDENCE
CREATION

with Him as *the Father* that we can understand why He created man and all things necessary for His family. There are certain naturalists and some secret orders who have built an entire religious system around the glory and majesty of God's creative handiwork. Nature, they insist, is God revealed. But the works of His hands are only intended to lead us to Him that we may worship Him and not His works.

There are others who misappropriate the *providential strand*. They would make it appear that God is just a great Santa Claus who waits on man and provides all his needs. They know He is a "good God" but never really understand the basis of His providential activity. Until they see how the Father has provided not only through the natural order for His created family, but how much more intimately He works with His begotten children, they will always misinterpret this providential strand and fail to see how it is integrated into the whole Paternal intention.

Others are prone to overemphasize the *governmental strand,* as though the establishment of the kingdom and righteous government were the primary program of God. To be sure it is an important means—a part, yet it is not the whole. Only as we see God chiefly as THE FATHER can we understand the proper place which government plays in His family. Then we neither neglect nor overemphasize government, but realize it is only a means of attaining His ultimate intention in His family. Today we are well aware that those who make the state or government to be the end interpret man as a mere pawn existing for the state.

But perhaps the vast majority in Christendom have almost unwittingly made the *redemptive strand* to be the whole cord—at least the one around which all other elements of God's purpose are woven. How distorted things then become! We can only see redemption in its highest glory when it is a Father who redeems man so as to fulfill His original purpose. Furthermore we know that our heavenly Father could not have

planned for the Fall just so He could redeem man. We need only look
back into His Father-heart to see that from eternity there always
existed the full capacity for redemption. It was a strand already there
to be uncovered as the need might arise when man turned to "his own
way." From God's standpoint it was already in the eternal plan, but
from ours—it awaited man's moral choice. Thus we see how the redemptive strand plays an important part, yet is only a means and certainly not the end God had in view. Why then, do we preach—if not in
doctrine, at least by inference—as though redemption is the only theme
in God's economy?

Even sanctification as a strand has an eternal aspect as well as a
sequence in time. It was from the beginning that the Father chose to
set apart for Himself those whom He had marked out to be adult sons.
Even so He determined that His created son, Adam, might in the fulness
of time come to a begotten relationship and enjoy the privilege of
sharing the divine or uncreated life of the Father through the Son. It
was the Father's intention that Adam might not only share His image
and likeness, but also share His very life, spirit, nature and mind. In
sharing these, Adam might by his own response set himself apart unto
the divine intention for which he was set apart by God in the beginning.
In this manner he could have become the glorious means for revealing
the eternal Father, even as the Lord Jesus in due time came to make
that glorious revelation.

ONLY MEANS AND METHODS

Now all these strands which become the subject matter for our
lessons: creation, providence, government, sanctification, begetting
and finally revelation—all are important means and methods by which
the Father will realize His ultimate intention. How perfectly they blend
together—in the eternal outlook—though in time we have separated them
so that we might understand them individually.

With this larger view of the *ultimate Paternal theme* we see how life
can be measured in four dimensions. First, there is the length of life—
it is not important how long we live, but that we live in the Eternal
with the comprehension of His viewpoint. Second, there is the breadth—
or how fully or interestingly we live. In discovering the Father's
ultimate dedication, we become gripped, even as was the Lord Jesus,
by a supreme dedication to help Him realize all His Father-heart yearns
for. What could be more interesting? Third, we understand the depth of
life to be the devotedness with which we live. We can measure this

too, for it is not merely a devotion to a project or cause—nor to what we can get out of life—but to a Person. Depth is determined by how we live unto Him.

Then there is that mysterious fourth dimension which we might call the purpose of life—or why we live. Apart from an unveiling of His FATHER-HEART there could be no ultimate living. There would be no way to measure what is truly ultimate. Why did He create? Why does He provide? Why does He rule? Why did He incorporate redemption? Why did He "set us apart" in the eternal past? Why did He plan for our spiritual begetting? Why was God's revelation of Himself so imperative? Surely it is only as we begin living in the eternal, sharing His supreme dedication, sharing His utter devotion and His ultimate intention—that we know the ultimate dimensions of life. But all that that means can only unfold as we see things "steadily from His viewpoint and see them related to the whole."

WHILE MEN are engulfed in the part—salvation, suffering, sin and tragedy—it is often difficult to see the whole: His purpose. Yet God is ever seeking to lift everyone to an intimate awareness of His ultimate intention which transcends suffering and transmutes it into a participation in a greater fellowship in God that is creative, purposeful and ultimate. This means truly . . .

Living for the Whole

ONE MORNING I went to the back door to call our three-year-old son. I planned for him to go with me to town on an errand. As I opened the back door to call, I saw him—but what a predicament he was in. The little fellow had been playing in the garden and had fallen in the mud. So as I called him it was now with a two-fold purpose: there was the overshadowing purpose—taking him to town with me; but there was also the incidental need of "washing up" which must be incorporated into the purpose. I must first minister some "grace" so that my purpose could be fulfilled.

After I had cleaned him up and changed his clothes, the little fellow attached himself to a new toy which he had just received. Immediately he became so engrossed in playing that he was completely lost to the real purpose for which I had called him in. He enjoyed being delivered from his muddy predicament, and dressed in clean clothes, but seemed wholly unconcerned about my original purpose. "Daddy," he insisted, "Let me stay home and play."

Suddenly I realized how easily God's children can partake of His "grace" and receive His good gifts only to become wholly distracted from His original purpose. It reminded me of Paul's significant statement to Timothy, his young son in the faith, "(God) hath saved us, and called us with an holy calling, not according to our works, but according to HIS OWN PURPOSE AND GRACE, which was given us in Christ Jesus before the world began" (2 Tim. 1:8-9).

We notice that God's calling is now twofold: "according to . . . *purpose* and *grace.*" The apostle knows that Timothy must be identified with God in His eternal purpose if he is to stand in the midst of afflictions and pressures. Thus he exhorts Timothy to recognize that he is not merely called "according to the grace of God," but he also is called "according to (God's) own purpose."

Although God knew from the very beginning that Adam would take the downward turn, and it would be necessary to incorporate the ministry of grace, we can be sure He did not intend that fallen man should become so enamored with the "calling of grace" that he would overlook the call to realize God's purpose. Yet, this has been the inner perversion of all Adam's fallen sons. Man is ever prone to interpret God's work as it benefits and relates to him, without concern for the realization of the yearning desire hidden in the Father-heart.

TAKING THE PART FOR THE WHOLE

Perhaps the blackboard drawing will clarify the reason for this perversion which appears even among those who despise this selfish man-centered approach to life.

Suppose you were starting on a long trip ("A" to "Z") to reach a certain destination. But at junction "W" you took the wrong road and driving on, unconscious of your lost predicament, at "X" you suddenly found yourself far from the main road. Upon inquiry, you learned there was a beautiful road ("X" to "Y") leading back to the main highway. When you reach "Y" on the main highway, you are overcome with the beauty of the road by which you returned to the original route, so there you camp and spend the day telling everyone of the "way" out. A week later you are still there telling your great experience of getting out of a lost condition. A year later, ten years later, you are still there telling all who will listen about your wrong-road experience and the wonderful way out.

Somehow in all of this, "Y" became the goal when it was really only a gateway to the ultimate destination. You allowed the "off-road

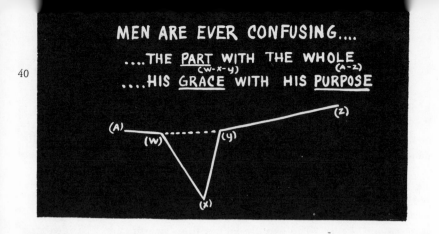

MEN ARE EVER CONFUSING....

....THE PART WITH THE WHOLE
(w-x-y)   (A-z)
....HIS GRACE WITH HIS PURPOSE

experience" to overshadow the purpose of the entire trip. Thus the part became the whole. You forgot that there was another purpose for the journey and another destination.

Homely as this illustration may be (and don't attempt to make it fit every detail), it gives a graphic picture of how the redemptive phase of God's grace may be allowed to overshadow God's original intention. What nearsightedness this causes—this interpreting of God's purposes as they are related to us and our welfare.

Who could rightly say that redemption was intended to be the central theme of God's universe any more than we would insist the off-road experience was the whole trip? Of course not! Before redemption ever became necessary, the Father had an original purpose which did not necessitate redemption for its realization. However precious and wonderful redemption may be to fallen, wayward humanity, it is only one phase of God's great plan. God did not plan that man must sin, so that He could use redemption as the glorious means of demonstrating His grace. God's purpose in calling is much greater.

But it would be equally wrong to assume that God was caught off-guard in man's fall and that redemption was but an afterthought. Surely His foreknowledge comprehended full-well what man as a moral agent would do. Thus long before Adam was created or before he sinned and turned to his own way, God perfectly incorporated the glorious means of redemption into His plan and thereby demonstrates the "riches of His grace." Thus God could remind us that "Jesus Christ was the Lamb slain from the foundation of the world" (Rev. 13:8). ". . . who verily was foreordained before the foundation of the world, but was manifest in these last times for you" (1 Pet. 1:20).

CALLED TO ULTIMATE FELLOWSHIP

Finally we must recognize that God's calling is to a glorious participation, not in mere parts, but in the whole. And this participation of fellowship (same word: *koinonia* in the Greek) is always up to the measure or level of our experience or revelation. Sometimes we think it is difficult for us to find much fellowship with those whose interests are so different from ours. What about God, who seeks to fellowship with man, yet finds him centered in himself and his own little purposes?

So our Father is ever seeking to move man beyond the shallows to the ocean depth itself—from living only in *our purposes*, to become alive to *His purposes*. Notice the progression of our fellowship with Him and with others. First, we are called into the "fellowship in the gospel" (Phil. 1:5). This is wonderful, for we share in the common experience of God's wonderful grace. But it is only a beginning. Then as we learn to walk we are led into the "fellowship of the Spirit" (Phil. 2:1), and thus we recognize the call to walk after and be filled with the Spirit. But the Holy Spirit lives only to make Christ more real and so we are called into a (deeper) "fellowship with His Son" (1 Cor. 1:9). What could be more wonderful? But as we share His mind and grow in this fellowship we are, like Paul, called into a "fellowship of His sufferings" (Phil. 3:10). Here is the call to those who would enter into a fruitful ministry, like the Lord Jesus, living unto the Father and sharing His resurrection power and authority.

We are convinced that none will continue long in this "fellowship of sufferings" unless they have, as Paul exhorted Timothy, moved into a larger fellowship in the Father-Himself and His own purposes. Accordingly, Paul unveils his own deepest concern in calling "all men to see what is the fellowship of the mystery" (Eph. 3:9). Here is the ultimate in fellowship. Yet there are many who are content to leave it a mystery. They have never realized there is a participation in the Father whereby we might share in that "which from the beginning has been hid in God." But now, Paul reminds us, it is God's intention to "make known by the church His manifold wisdom." Surely this is His call to the Church to live in the eternal, to participate in the glorious purposes and intention of God. It means that we should live where all the parts find their perfect integration into the whole—His intention.

One casual look around us in the church today reveals that men have become occupied with various parts of truth. Truth thus accepted determines the level of their fellowship. Some read the Bible as though it were only a book of salvation. Thank God it is that—but it is more. Others read it as though it were merely the "book of the kingdom." It includes that—but much more. "In other words," says R. B. Jones, "It reveals the ultimate purposes of God in Christ. It also shows some of the ways by which Satan has hoped to thwart God in the attaining of

His ultimate purpose, His GRAND END. The salvation of men is not an end in itself. Neither Israel nor the Church represent the *ultimate* in God's purpose. These are rather parts of a great plan; some of the things incidental to a design mightier and more magnificent even than that found in themselves. To fail to recognize this is indicative of serious defect in spiritual vision."

What does all this mean? Simply that we must move to a God-centered position from which we can properly understand the whole and relate all the parts. Simply that we cannot long fellowship with the Son and share in His dedication and sufferings before we shall come to a revelation of the Father such as we have never known. This is the Son's greatest delight: revealing Him. Then we shall find our basis of fellowship with the Father becomes an expanding, growing participation as we learn all that He has ultimately intended for Himself, for His only begotten Son, and for His many sons. What an invitation! To live in such unspeakable fellowship, participating in *the ultimate*. We shall see what it means.

$$\textcircled{5}$$

IT WOULD indeed be wonderful if we could live, as some have sought to do, in the delusion that there really was no Fall and, therefore, is no sin. But we know better. Sin is a reality—we all bear the marks of the Fall. Hence we must consider how God makes provision to lift the sinner out of his man-centered universe into a God-centered position. We shall see how the work of the Cross moves man from the old center . . . .

To A New Center

A FRIEND OF MINE has recently printed a little motto which reads: KEEP LOOKING DOWN. It of course causes no little comment from those who are accustomed to the phrase: KEEP LOOKING UP. The shock most often achieves its intention. If the observer is a believer, it serves to remind him that it does make a difference where he is positioned. If down here, of course we must *look up to Him.* But if we have truly entered into all that our position "with Christ in God" means, we have risen to a heavenly vantage point from which to view a whole new life.

A simple story will illustrate this. Little Billy promised faithfully that he would not leave the yard. He was reminded there would be throngs of people on the street that day to watch the parade. But once the bands started playing and the floats began moving by, he suddenly realized what he was missing. Oh, to be free of the tall board fence that surrounded the safety of his yard! All Billy could see of the parade was through a small knot hole in the board fence. People were constantly getting in his way.

Then he heard the voice of his big brother calling from the upstairs veranda, "Billy, why don't you come up here." Billy couldn't quite reach the bottom rung of the outside ladder, so his brother came down, lifted him in one strong arm and carried him to the top.

Of course! Here was the place to see everything! He looked down at the wide avenue from one end to the other. He thrilled with excitement. "Oh," he cried, "Now I can even see what went before, and what's passing now, and way up the street I can see what's coming. It's like living in a new world."

For Billy the past, present and future had come to blend into one big *now*. So it is when we come by God's invitation to view the parade of time from the heavenly vantage point. God not only sees in one vast sweep the events of time; He sees all He had planned before the book of Genesis began and all that will be consummated after the Revelation. As viewed from His *eternal now*, eternity becomes one complete whole with the span we call time as but a minute parenthesis.

It would seem the Psalmist must have been desirous of this heavenly position when he wrote: "The Lord looked down from heaven upon the children of men, to see if there were any that did *understand* and seek God." Understand! What? Did the Psalmist sense our need to look out from God's viewpoint before we could understand all He intended? But it is really the Apostle Paul who considers this viewpoint imperative. In his prayer for the Colossians, as given in Phillip's translation, he makes this thought clear: "We are asking God THAT YOU MAY SEE THINGS as it were FROM HIS POINT OF VIEW, by being given spiritual insight and understanding..." (Col. 1:9).

Thus every man is either still centered in himself, "looking up"

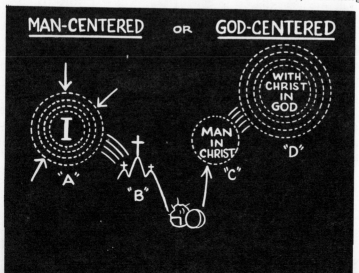

MAN-CENTERED   OR   GOD-CENTERED

from his own viewpoint, or he is enjoying the viewpoint Paul prayed about: He is "looking down" from God's vantage point—looking out through His eyes.

But mere wishful thinking will not move fallen man into this new position. It is not man's doing, but God's. It was God who entered into humanity completely enough to raise man to another plane of life, to deliver manhood into a new center where all things become new. On the blackboard we have pictured the means by which God translates man from the family of Adam into the kingdom of His Son.

"A" illustrates *all men in Adam* as they live unto themselves, relating all life's happenings to self. Instead of enthroning God, Adam enthroned himself by deliberately eating of the forbidden fruit. From that time everything has been out of order for Adam's entire family. By attempting to be ultimate himself, man seeks to use God and relate all His works for his own desires.

God expresses man's predicament in this way: "Destruction and misery are in their ways. "—not as a result of their ways but inherently *"in their ways."* Nothing will come out right for the person who either consciously or subconsciously makes the universe to revolve around himself. What a penalty, to live with a self you can't live with! As long as you center in yourself, you won't like yourself. Another has put it this way. "It's so wonderful to get yourself off your own hands and into the hands of God. It's like living in a new world!"

Man was not created to be the *center* and any attempt to build this false universe will only cause confusion. God has made life that way, and there is no use kicking against the goad, as Paul did to his hurt.

"B" illustrates how God, through the work of Christ on the Cross, has put an end to the old race of Adam. Paul explains it this way, "We thus judge, that one died for all, therefore all died; and he died for all, that they which live *should no longer live unto themselves*, but unto Him who for them died and rose again" (2 Cor. 5:14-15).

Paul reveals that it was God's purpose to take all of Adam's race to the Cross in order to deal with the "I" principle that stands in opposition to God. So when God looked down upon the Cross, He saw us united in death with His Son. All that is involved in the treachery of S-I-N (Selfish, Independent, Negation) is dealt with there. Thus from God's viewpoint man was crucified *with Christ*—but more. He was buried *with Christ* in Joseph's new tomb. Yet even more, he was raised *with Christ* to newness of life. But still more than that, he was positioned with Christ in God in a new heavenly position.

Now all this which God reckons to have happened as He sees it *from His viewpoint*, we must likewise reckon to be our experience by faith-appropriation. So Paul describes it in four words: *crucified, buried, risen* and *ascended*. This is not something we do. No, we see it by revelation—see that it happened to us "in Him"—and we by faith live in that reckoning.

"C" illustrates how man has been raised with Christ and is now in a new position "in Him." We know of multitudes of believers who have been well-taught about their *position in Christ*. They speak with conviction of the finished work by which they have forgiveness, deliverance, victory and authority. And well they might rejoice in all that has been done *for them*. Yet here is just the trouble—the snare. They have never changed centers. All that has been made available to them in Christ they continue to relate to themselves: the old center. They have missed the deepest severing power of the Cross which would deliver them to a life centered in God where all things are related *to Him*.

For almost fifteen years this writer preached the *glories of our position in Christ* and emphasized the truths of identification in the death and resurrection of Christ as this made available a victorious walk—a truth which is now being taught by hundreds throughout the country. Yet, I was, without realizing it always relating all this to man and his needs and welfare. It was all *for man*—what man received through his new position in Christ. Thus the center had not really changed.

Then one day the truth exploded. I realized just how short this was of bringing man to a full and total emancipation from his man-centeredness whereby he could live a whole, new life with a new center of relatedness. It became evident as long as one is still appealing to man *for what man can get,* it still fits into the popular approach. But it is a vastly different thing to experience the radical working of the Cross which liberates one from self to a new center. As long as one is still more alive to what God does for man, to what the Cross realizes for man, to what our position in Christ means for man—that individual has never grasped the Father's full intention for placing us in His Son: that we might come to the same vision, purpose, dedication and philosophy of life as the Son shares in the Father.

"D" illustrates what it means to live with an utterly new center of gravity. We are not merely centered "in Christ" but with Him are centered in God the Father. As we shall see, in this God-centered position it is no longer our victory, but living in His victory; it is no longer our purpose, but living in His purpose: it is no longer our dedication, but living in His dedication. All things have truly become new.

AS PICTURED on the previous blackboard the vast majority of believers stop at "C" where they seek to enjoy all that comes to them through their position "in Christ." They hear the cry, "possess your possessions," "live in your full inheritance." But soon many wonder why their attempt to appropriate all their blessings leaves them cold, empty and dissatisfied. It is because the full light has not dawned. God is not calling them to a life of getting but instead to be centered in Him where all is giving, where . . .

All Things Are New

IN SECOND CORINTHIANS, chapter 5, Paul seems to share the very heart of the issue. He explains what caused him to live a completely God-centered life. With Paul, being a new creature in Christ was more than a doctrinal position; it was an actual experience which became real by revelation. To be with Christ in God meant to look out through God's eyes, to see and interpret and relate all things to Him. One who has entered into this experience needs no one to explain it to him. He knows what it means to be released from the captivity of the old-world-center where all was self-relating and to be translated into a new world where all is God-related.

"Therefore if any man be IN CHRIST, he is a new creature; old things are passed away, BEHOLD ALL THINGS ARE BECOME NEW" (2 Cor. 5:17).

Let us consider four of the changes this will bring as we begin to look out *through His eyes* and appreciate all things as they work to realize His ultimate intention.

A NEW VIEWPOINT. In 2 Corinthians 5:16 Paul writes: "... from now on we estimate and regard no one from a [purely] human point of view—in terms of natural standards of value. [No] even though we once did estimate Christ from a human viewpoint... we know him [thus] no longer... "   (A.N.T.).

Once we looked at our own weakness and failure and it only brought despair. Once we lived under the scrutinizing eyes of others and it only brought bondage. Now we look out through His eyes and behold the rough stone upon which He is working—but we also see beyond to the finished product which He will make. We see ourselves as He sees us— not the rough stone, but the finished stone which will bring delight to Him.

What a difference! Seeing ourselves and others, no longer after the flesh, but seeing as God sees the living stones He will fit into the Temple of the Ages. How small this makes our wishes and our problems! Yet how great to be a part of something so tremendous as His ultimate intention.

A NEW RELATEDNESS. From this new viewpoint we begin to see with Paul, how all things work according to God's purpose. Previously we might have related events to ourselves and considered them as they affected us, but now we see them as related to His ultimate intention. So we say with Paul, "All things are of God..." (2 Cor. 5:18).

One night a veteran missionary on furlough sat with us before the fireplace. She told how God had prepared her heart to move away from a self-centered to a God-centered life. She explained how for several years she bit her lip when pressures or problems came and inwardly groaned, "Well, Lord, you know about this. I am sure 'all things work together for (my) good.' So I guess I can endure, since it will eventually work out for my benefit."

Then she continued, "Tonight, I've entered a new life with a new relatedness." She went on to explain how for years she had been a victim (unconsciously) of self-reference. She saw everything as it related to her and trusted all to work out eventually for her own good! "How much," she confessed, "I've been the center of my little religious world. Without realizing it, I have been trying to use God and interpret the bitter experiences just for me. I always meant well, but I have been utterly blind.

"Tonight I have come to see the great difference between being

occupied with God Himself, instead of with myself. The Holy Spirit has unveiled to me what Paul meant when from his new viewpoint he related all to God: 'I would that ye should understand brethren, that the things which have happened unto me have fallen out rather *unto the furtherance of the gospel.'*"

What an emancipation! When we begin to relate all the parts to the whole we will see how God is doing everything with a perfect relatedness to that desire He has purposed in Himself.

A NEW OCCUPATION. Paul further reminds us in 2 Corinthians 5:20, "...so we are Christ's Ambassadors, God making His appeal through us...." The songwriter who understood something of this new position put it thus: "Once I tried to use Him, now He uses me." Once we were occupied with working *for Him.* Now we are occupied *with Him* and He works through us.

So it is the new man "in Him" who clearly understands his separation unto God. He refuses to meet men any longer on the ground of the flesh. Now as Christ's personal representatives this is our message: "We beg you *for His sake,* to lay hold of divine favor...." No longer do we appeal to men merely *for their own sake,* but rather *for His sake.* Only from this new viewpoint do we understand our new occupation: We are first occupied with a Person, then with His purpose; first with worship and then with His work.

A NEW YARDSTICK. So much is being said these days about being adjusted to God, and coming into harmony with Him. But with what shall we measure? Adjusted—but to what?

Too much of the preaching about reconciliation has been reconciliation *to God*—but wholly for ourselves. Surely Paul has much more in view when he says, (vs 18): "... God, reconciled us to Himself (brought us into harmony with Himself) and gave to us the ministry of reconciliation that by word and deed we might bring others into harmony with Him" A.N.T.

The question is: What is the yardstick for measuring whether we are fulfilling or falling short of God's purpose? We can only be in full harmony with the Father as we are dedicated to and living for the same thing: HIS ULTIMATE INTENTION.

It is imperative to recognize that the Father has purposed at least three things FOR HIS SON. Let us see the several phrases which, when pieced together, give us the full picture of this intention.

(1) Paul speaks of "my knowledge in the mystery of Christ" (Eph. 3:4). What was that mystery? It was that the Son might have a corporate Body through which to express Himself. It is this mystery of Christ in you—the means by which God's glory shall be manifest in every believer. (Col. 1:27).

(2) Again, it is the Father's intention that His Son shall be the Head of this Body, the altogether pre-eminent One who expresses not only Himself, but the fulness of the Godhead. Thus the Father and the Holy Spirit also are revealed and expressed throughout the whole universe by the lives of His many sons. (Col. 1:18).

(3) Further, the Father has intended to make Him (the Son) to be the center and gathering point for all things in heaven and earth—"to sum up all things in Christ" (Eph. 1:10). All things were not only created "by Him," but "FOR HIM" (Col. 1:16).

What a glorious unveiling—almost beyond our comprehension. To think that the Father hath purposed in Himself to make Christ the *center* of His working. The altogether lovely One, His Son, is to have the pre-eminence.

Knowing this ultimate intention for the Son we can better understand the Father's intention for His many sons who make up Christ's Body.

Now we can recognize that whatever comes short of revealing *that which the Father ultimately intends for His Son* is just *short*—it needs to be rectified, brought into harmony. Looking out from His Father-heart we now have the ultimate yardstick by which we can measure things which fulfill or fall short of the Father's intention. Everything that harmonizes with this has His approval.

To some it may seem strange that the Father would dedicate Himself to such an end. Yet, that is what He has purposed in Himself from the counsels of eternity past. But let us remember, the eternal Son and His Body of rectified sons are destined to live for one thing: The most complete and supreme honor, glory, pleasure and satisfaction which they can bring to the heavenly Father. So while the Father is concerned for His Son, the Son is also concerned for the Father. As we shall see in the coming lessons this is the divine rule of action which governs all heaven. It is His intention that all His sons shall be invited to embrace this divine purpose and philosophy of life.

WE HAVE SEEN how many would use the Cross for their
own ends, and thus miss God's ultimate intention in the
Cross. In the coming chapters we must see how the
Cross brings a radical new perspective which means an
utter rectification. For the Cross has not wrought its
deepest work until we move beyond interpreting what
Christ did "for us" and begin to see what it realized
"for God." Only then can we say we are truly positioned
with Christ in God where we live in the reality of . . .

A Divine Rectification

FOR SEVERAL YEARS this writer has longed to delve more deeply
into Romans 3:23—a verse which is often used so glibly—for it seemed
to contain a larger meaning that God intended for us to know. The King
James translation reads: "All have sinned and come short of the glory
of God."

What was that glory of which men had come short? J. B. Phillips
seemed to sense the need to shed more light on this and so put it:
"All have sinned and missed the beauty of God's plan." Then we
discovered that Ferrar Fenton translated it thus: "All sin and are in
need of RECTIFICATION." Here was another attempt to give more
comprehensive meaning. Fenton was sure Paul was expressing God's
highest concern that man come to a complete and ultimate rectification
to God's plan and intention. Paul realized that man needed more than a
moral and mental, a physical and spiritual rectification. His deepest

need could be met only as he had a *philosophical* rectification. In other words the purpose for which man lives is the mainspring. This must be right or all else will surely be wrong. Nothing less than a philosophical rectification which adjusts man in his motive, purpose and vision will produce a proper relatedness and power to fulfill the divine intention.

Many may be concerned by the use of the term philosophy. There is a vain philosophy of this world which we are warned to avoid, but there is also a *divine philosophy*. The very fact God made man with a deep gnawing in his bosom which longs to know *why—why*, demonstrates that man is born a philosopher. Failure to properly answer the philosophical gnawing in man's breast is causing fundamentalists by the hundreds to become fertile soil for the *false* philosophies of this world.

As we have said, God's answer to man's need is not a philosophy, but a Person. Paul knew better than to meet the Corinthians on the level of human philosophy. Instead, he preached what was to them an obnoxious message—Christ crucified. God used this message to manifest His power. He used that which seemed like utter foolishness to uncover their pride of intellect and man-centered wisdom. Such is God's way. We present a Person, Jesus Christ, who becomes a divine (philosophy) way of life in us.

It is not a coincidence that God has intended for man to have this necessary wisdom by which to chart the course and purpose of life. God knew from the beginning that he would need a divine wisdom (philosophy) which alone could complete his rectification. Thus we read in 1 Corinthians 1:30: "But from Him you exist in Christ Jesus who has brought a PHILOSOPHY from God to us—as well as righteousness, purity and redemption" (F. Fenton).

Oh may God help us to see it! Here is God's means for a complete rectification. But we must be careful at this point or we shall fall into the traditional snare. If we interpret this verse (1:30) in the light of how "wisdom, righteousness, sanctification and redemption" will benefit us, we are still man-centered and have missed God's intention. But to have moved into a God-centered position is to interpret this as realizing for God. What a difference it makes! Through redemption I belong to Him, not to myself—He paid the price. This becomes my new viewpoint. Through sanctification I am set apart *unto Him*. This brings a new relatedness. Through His righteousness I come into complete harmony and a right standing with Him. This means my new occupation. Through a divine philosophy I now share heaven's pattern and purpose of life.

So this rectification to a divine philosophy is not something I get, but a new sphere—a new world I am called to enter. Paul seemed to realize how blind the religious leaders were to the divine philosophy by which God intended to accomplish a total rectification. He said to the Corinthians (1 Cor. 2:6-8):

"But we can speak philosophy among the perfect; but a philosophy not of this age, nor of the useless leaders of this time. We speak instead, a divine philosophy in the hidden mystery which God ordained before the ages FOR OUR RECTIFICATION, which none of the leaders of this age recognized; for if they had recognized, they would not have crucified the MASTER OF THAT RECTIFICATION" (F. Fenton).

We can be sure it is the same today. Religious leaders have missed the true intention of His coming. As in that day they only wanted to use Him, so today they would use Him, but deny the divine way of life He came to implant and make operative in lives.

How can we better express this divine way of life (philosophy) than to repeat: The Father purposes in Himself for all things to be centered in His Son. But the Son in turn dedicates Himself to reveal, glorify and satisfy the Father. While universal dominion is an ultimate intention of the Father for His Son, we read in 1 Corinthians 15:24 and 28 that when all things are under the rule of the Son, He will turn them over to His Father. Each living unto the Other. It is this *divine rule of action* which the Father intends to make operative in all His family.

Through the centuries men have marveled at the dedication and insight of the Apostle Paul. What was the secret of his life and ministry? He indicated what it was in a most decisive way. Listen to the throbbing of his heart as he explains the rule of action which governs his life:

"... whatever we do is either FOR GOD or for others. If we are

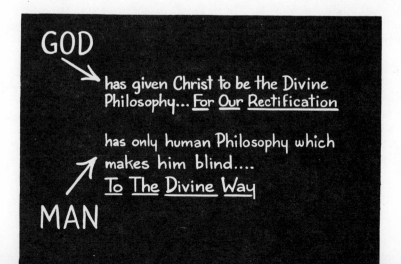

GOD has given Christ to be the Divine Philosophy... For Our Rectification

has only human Philosophy which makes him blind.... To The Divine Way

MAN

*beside ourselves [mad, as some say] it is FOR GOD and concerns Him;
if we are in our right mind, it is FOR YOUR BENEFIT"* (2 Cor. 5:13:
A.N.T.).

Of this one thing we can be sure. Here is one who has been lifted
out of his man-centered philosophy of living into the God-centered
philosophy of living. When we live no longer *unto* or *for* ourselves, but
to and *for* Him, it is then "old things have become new!"

Here is rectification! Nothing less than a glimpse of the Father's
ultimate intention could have held Paul in such vigorous ministry;
nothing else could have supplied such motivating power. Why have we
missed it so long?

*"Now I rejoice for your sake in sufferings, and would fill up in my
body the extreme of Christ's afflictions for the sake of His body—the
church..."* (Col. 1:24 F. Fenton).

There is no attempt to escape from hardship and suffering nor
indulge in self-pity. Paul had his eye on the *many membered Body*
which would someday embrace the divine rule of action and extend its
operation throughout the whole universe. In Colossians 1:25-27 he
writes:

*"... of which I became a minister by appointment given to me for
you from God, to accomplish the DIVINE INTENTION, the secret hidden
from the ages, and from the nations, but now made manifest to His
saints by whom God has decided to publish amongst the heathen what
is the wealth of that mystery of the RECTIFICATION which Christ is
to you—the hope of the rectification—which we proclaim..."* (F.
Fenton).

May I pause here again to draw your attention to Paul's complete
concern for the divine intention. He was living that God might realize
through him; not, as so many with a man-centered vision who are living
for what might be done *for them.* There is a difference. Of course he
realized that the basis for our being poured out for Him springs from a
proper philosophy. He continues:

*"... warning every man, and teaching every person in a perfect
philosophy, so that we may present each one perfect in Christ; to which
object I vigorously strive with His mighty energy working in me"*
(Col. 1:28-29 F. Fenton).

At last we have reached that point in this book where we can say,
here is THE OBJECT AND PURPOSE OF OUR WRITING: To bring
everyone to that same vision and purpose that they may live unto God
and His ultimate intention. Oh God, may it be so.

8

AS WE LOOK out from our Paternal viewpoint we are amazed to discover that the Cross is eternal in God. In fact it clearly demonstrates this DIVINE RULE OF ACTION which operates in the God-head and which is The Father's . . .

Ultimate Intention for Man

IF YOU HAD one son in whom you found unspeakable delight, would it not be normal as a father to want many more? It is exactly so with the eternal Father, who by nature and choice, has desired and purposed to have a vast family of human-divine sons who are just like His only begotten Son.

Further, as we view from His heart, it seems evident that the Father makes all His plans with His eternal Son in view; that in the unfolding ages ahead, Jesus Christ might have a glorious Body in which to express His very life, and a family of brothers with whom He might enjoy fellowship.

Then as we understand the innermost purpose of the Son, we see how in turn He dedicates Himself to helping the Father realize His intention for Himself; that He (the Father) might have a family of sons in whom He can have paternal honor, glory, pleasure and delight. The Father plans for His Son, whereas the Son lives unto the Father.

So it is in the Godhead. In a sense no member lives *for* or *unto Himself*, but each for the Other. The Father intends that in all things the Son might have pre-eminence. The Son lives to reveal the Father and thus brings glory and pleasure to Him. Likewise the Spirit speaks not of Himself (nor for Himself) but dedicates His activity to the revealing of the Son and to realizing for both the Father and Son.

What is this inner attitude, spirit and purpose of selfless giving, serving and sharing but a *divine rule of action* which has always been expressive in God? This is the principle revealed in the Cross.

THE ETERNAL CROSS

It may come as a real surprise to some when we suggest that the Cross has always been an eternal principle in God. It is not an after thought or accident in the universe, nor is it a principle read into things by loving hearts. It is inherent in God. This Cross-principle which seems woven into the very bosom of the Father is demonstrated by the Son and interpreted by the Spirit. It has ever been the principle of action by which the Godhead would surely bring to pass the divine intention.

We see then the Cross is far more than an act in history. It expresses the very qualities and manner of life of the triune God. It is the life-giving, light-sharing and love-bestowing principle by which God has dealt with man from the beginning.

Now let us see (as on the blackboard) how this *eternal Cross in God* was to become the *inwrought Cross in man.* Only when man refused this, was it necessary for an outward demonstration of the *historic Cross on Golgotha.*

GOD'S PLAN FOR THE INWROUGHT CROSS

In thinking of the Cross only as a redemptive measure, we have missed God's larger intention. Yet the total inference of Scripture is that from the beginning the Father longed for a family of sons who would embrace the same Cross-principle that has ever governed His own heart. It was His intention that the Cross might be so inwrought in these sons as to become their manner and purpose of life. And until this giving and sharing can be accomplished in man there is no real basis of fellowship for God and man.

But we might ask, "How much did the first man, Adam, know of God's intention for him?"

Once again it becomes evident that when we begin at the right place—in the Paternal Heart—we shall always see in God's larger perspective. The Cross which has usually appeared only redemptive becomes more—It becomes expressive of God's manner of life which

He intends in due time to be reflected everywhere in the universe.

From our present viewpoint we know that the Father was inviting Adam to embrace the Cross-principle as the manner and purpose of his life. This, however, could not be thrust upon him, but must come as the exercise of moral choice—the choice of living to give, to serve, and thus, to share. We are sure that God was waiting to make a fuller disclosure of His inner being which would have unfolded more and more as Adam went from obedience to obedience.

Had Adam chosen the divine intention for his life—a choice represented in the two trees—then through each successive choice this divine way of life would have been more fully inwrought in him. His first choice of the Cross, as an operating principle, would call for a continued ratifying to make it an operating practice in his daily walk. Thus God and man would have become two hearts living in complete harmony.

When God first presented His intention to Adam, it was simple—easy to understand. Adam was to enter into the highest calling open to man: He was to be a father who would fill the whole earth after his kind; then as a paternal king, he was to rule over all.

Would he choose God's intention or pursue a private goal? This was the great issue. For Adam, who stood in pristine neutrality, to choose God's intention would mean the yielding back to Him of his very right to life, liberty and the pursuit of happiness and to come under the divine government and purpose.

Choosing *his own way* meant that Adam would feed upon the tree of knowledge and thereby develop his natural life, excerise his own rights to freedom, and pursue his own private goal. By choosing God's intention and sacrificing the natural, Adam might have entered into

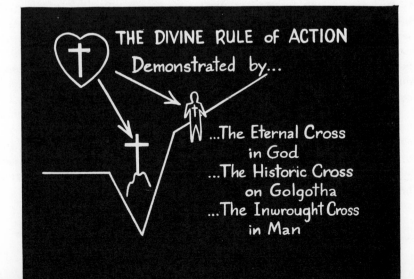

THE DIVINE RULE of ACTION
Demonstrated by...

...The Eternal Cross
in God
...The Historic Cross
on Golgotha
...The Inwrought Cross
in Man

God's own life and into true liberty. He could have partaken of God's *tree of life,* God's provision for realizing the divine goal and intention.

So the first Adam stood at the gateway of choice. Would he accept God's call to embrace the divine rule of action and allow the Cross-principle to be inwrought in him; or would he choose to live for his own purpose and thereby reject God's purpose?

WHY THE HISTORIC CROSS WAS NEEDED

We know, all too well, the way Adam chose. We realize how through his selfish choice he became blind to the heavenly way of life. Moreover, his posterity has ever since lived under a veil of darkness. Although the eternal Cross is everywhere written into the very fabric of the universe, blinded man, limited by sin and his natural senses, could not understand the Cross-principle of self-giving without an outward demonstration.

For this very reason the Father robed His Son in human flesh and sent Him to walk among men. Every step He took from the hour the Father attested to His Sonship at the River Jordan, was a revelation of this divine way of life. Immediately He was led into the wilderness where He met Satan and perfectly demonstrated what was to be His manner of life: He would do nothing *for Himself.* (He refused to make stones into bread.) He would do nothing *of Himself.* (He would not cast Himself down from the temple and use His power to save Himself.) He would do nothing *with Himself.* (Committed to His Father's purpose, He would not bow to the purpose of another.) Here in three simple prepositions: *for, of,* and *with* we have the clearest expression of the heavenly way of life.

So as a divine Invader of the human family, Jesus demonstrated heaven's way of *giving* to minds darkened by *grasping.* Every step along His earthly pilgrimage was a continuous conflict with the evil powers uncovered by His guileless simplicity. The world's great would not accept Him because of the way of life He represented. Having come to reveal His Father, He was also revealing them and they hated to be seen as they really were.

Now that we have this clearly before us, we can understand the many crosses strewn all along Jesus' route to Golgotha. All those who represented earth's way of saving one's life got crossed up. To blinded man He seemed to be a great "Crosser-upper"—though He really was the great "Harmonizer." In every such encounter there was a double exposure: the contrast between man's way and God's way.

In the wilderness He crossed Satan and unveiled his clever scheme of offering this world's kingdoms apart from the Cross. He crossed Peter and the disciples every time their self-saving purposes led them astray. He even crossed His own mother when she forgot her Son's divine mission and sought to press her motherly claims to His affection. Yes, He crossed the human grain of an entire race of fallen men and in anger they finally nailed Him to THE CROSS.

SHALL WE MISS HIS ULTIMATE INTENTION?

While we marvel at the blindness of those who made this fatal choice, we must be sure we have fully escaped their error. To interpret the redemptive work of the historic Cross only as a happy remedy for sin, and a source of blessing and power, may be just another example of this man-centered blindness. Alas, such a one has only seen the Cross as the answer to his own need. He has completely missed the eternal Cross which God intends to be inwrought in man. It is only as this inwrought principle of giving becomes operative that suddenly man becomes alive to all that God longs to realize in his life.

Throughout the following lessons we shall keep these two phases of the Cross clearly in mind. We shall see how the Holy Spirit interprets the historic Cross in its wonderful redemptive and rectifying work as it recovers man for God, but we shall also ever keep before us this overshadowing theme: it was and still is the Father's ultimate intention that He might have a vast family who embrace the inwrought-Cross which they have seen reflected from His paternal heart. Let us never forget that this Cross-principle was revealed in the Father-heart from eternity, long before the Cross of Christ (in time) made this principle redemptive. Our choice then, is either the Cross *for me*, or the Cross *in me for God*. Let us never stop short of His full intention.

9

LOOKING OUT from His paternal viewpoint we can better understand that no thing which God purposed and planned in the counsels of eternity is ever affected by time, by sin, or by the Fall. Because God is God, what He has purposed will come to pass. Isaiah the prophet speaks for Him: "For I am God . . . I have purposed it, I will also do it." Let us thus observe how . . .

The Father's Plan Unfolds

ON THE BLACKBOARD we have pictured four phases which God intends for each one to pass through. Unless we grasp the plan God has in view, we shall never clearly understand why these steps are necessary in accomplishing His end. They are best described in four phrases: "to be"—creaturehood; "to become"—sonship; "to share"—heirship; "to reign"—throneship.

First it is important to understand that Adam as he came from the creative hand of God did not have divine life. Although created sinless, intelligent and happy, the first man did not possess one tiny spark of the uncreated life of God. Biologically, man in the garden *was not* God's child. Only in a created sense could he be called the son of God.

God's own life is uncreated and eternal. Since Adam was but a created being, he was by God's intention only to have created life until such time as he might "become" a partaker of divine Life. Since human life comes from Adam, all men are creatures possessing nothing of God's eternal life in themselves. They might be called potential sons, for they are created with a spirit which may be kindled by the life of God. But only by exercising their power of choice in embracing God's way and manner of life, can they receive God's life and "become," through a begotten relationship, sons of God.

SOMETHING ADAM NEVER HAD

According to His pattern of working—first the natural and afterward the spiritual, first obedience, and then revelation—God could not thrust divine life upon Adam. The tree of life (typical of the life-giving, eternal Son) grew in the garden, but Adam had not yet discerned its supreme value.

It seems further evident then, that in the crowning act of creating Adam in His image and after His likeness, God endowed mankind with much more than the rest of His creation could enjoy. Yet, even with God, the creative process has its limitations. Adam was designed "to be" all that God could make him by His creative hand. God's divine life, His nature, His power and His throne could only be granted through other means. So the door was open for Adam "to become," "to share" and "to reign."

Let us realize then that even before Adam sinned, he needed a vital birth relationship in order *to become* a son according to the Father's plan. How different things look when we make this important discovery. The first Adam was created with natural life, i.e. "became a living soul," and only by a union with God could he experience uncreated life from Christ, the last Adam, who was sent as a "quickening Spirit."

Perhaps nothing has so blighted the vision and growth of believers as the false assumption that Adam in his innocence and sinless state was all that God ever purposed him to be. It is this error which leads many to believe that God's highest intention is to restore man's lost paradise. This kind of reasoning is the fruit of a wrong starting point.

In his book *The Normal Christian Life,* Watchman Nee confirms this truth:

What was (His) purpose? God wanted to have a race . . . whose members were gifted with a spirit whereby communion would be possible with Himself, who is Spirit. The race, possessing God's own life, was to cooperate in securing His purposed end by defeating every possible uprising of the enemy and undoing his evil works. . . . He is concerned with bringing us into, and bringing into us SOMETHING ADAM NEVER HAD. . . . It is something positive and purposive, going far beyond the recovery of a lost position.

THE FATHER'S ORIGINAL PLAN

It will be observed on the blackboard, we have not pictured the tragic dip downward as caused by the Fall. We have purposely omitted this to direct our attention to the original intention of the Father. His plan was not determined by sin, as so many unwittingly infer, but rather in the Father-heart, it was all in spite of sin.

From the beginning, we are sure, God intended for Adam (and his family) to develop morally, mentally and spiritually. We know that Adam was created perfect. By this we mean that he was without imperfections because he was the handiwork of God. He was perfect even as a little babe is perfect yet untried or undeveloped in moral or spiritual development which could only come through moral choices.

In referring to this Oswald Chambers suggests it was according to the plan of God that Adam, by a series of moral choices, would be required to take part in his own moral development; that is, "he was to transform the life of nature into the spiritual life by obeying God."

If Adam, created neutral, were voluntarily to turn God's way and choose dependence upon Him, he would thereby become able to receive of the tree of life (representing God's own life). God would then have a life-union with man—This is "sonship."

God's intended pathway for Adam was sonship, heirship and throne-ship. But these three phases of God's plan can only become real as His sons learn to be led by the Spirit, "For as many as are led by the Spirit of God, they are (mature) sons of God" (Rom. 8:14). From eternity, God's call to Adam and his posterity has been to enter into sonship which is the gateway to:

PARTICIPATION — in His very life and purpose,

APPROPRIATION — of all that God desires to share,

QUALIFYING — by discipline for the throne.

Notice as Paul arrives at Romans 8:14, after the early chapters have recovered man from his fallen condition, he is at the place where Adam could have been if he had entered upon the pathway of living for God's intention and purpose. It is indeed tragic that too many seem only interested in reaching this point. For with Paul, who understood the Father's intention, this is really the beginning point of realizing for God. Let us see how these three phases, *sonship*, *heirship* and *throneship* are to be worked out in the experience of every begotten son by the pathway of *participation*, *appropriation* and *qualifying*.

First, SONSHIP: In Romans 8:16, Paul points out that the Spirit witnesses to each when he is a child of God, "a born-one, *(teknon)."* This is the Father's desire, that the Spirit shall work in the newborn child to bring about full-sonship. "Beloved, we are [even here and] now God's children; it is not yet disclosed [made clear]what we shall be [hereafter], but we know that when He comes and is manifested we shall (as God's children) resemble and be like Him. . . . And everyone that hath this hope purifies himself. . ." (1 John 3:2, 3 A.N.T.).

We must be quick to discern that there are some things which only come as a gift from God—His life, His nature, His Spirit. But there are other things, such as Christ-like character, Christ's mind, vision, purpose and dedication, which are the product of training, overcoming, discipline, trial, hardship and intensive spiritual qualifying. All of this was according to God's original plan—not because man sinned, but even if he had not fallen.

Next, HEIRSHIP: In Romans 8:17, Paul writes of our joint-heirship with Christ. Birth relationship gives one the right to heirship, but participation in all heirship means, comes only to those who live unto the Father's intention.

When Alexander the Great was twelve years old, his father, King Philip of Macedonia, arranged for Aristotle to become his companion and tutor. Later Alexander claimed the great philosopher to be his "father." He meant, that while he had received his body from Philip, Aristotle was the father of his mind. Alexander said he was more grateful to Aristotle for knowledge than to Philip for life.

Even so we as sons of God by birth must choose whether we will allow our heavenly Father to impart to us His mind, purpose, vision and ultimate intention. There is much He longs to share with those who, by growth and development of character, are able to receive a

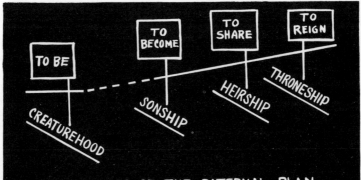

FOUR PHASES OF THE PATERNAL PLAN
WHICH HAVE NEVER CHANGED

diet of meat. He is ever waiting "till we all come in the unity of the faith, and of the knowledge of the Son of God, unto a perfect man, unto the measure of the stature of the fulness of Christ" (Eph. 4:13).

Even though we may forget God's intention for each son, He never does. And He leads us through a thousand experiences, incomprehensible when not viewed in the light of His purpose. Each crucible experience is designed to bring forth in us a fuller participation in heirship.

So let us keep this distinction in mind and not deceive ourselves by thinking because we have had certain genuine experiences, such as salvation, separation, consecration, filling of the Spirit or healing, that any one or all of these experiences can in themselves mean we have attained growth in stature or character. These are like a series of crises through which the Holy Spirit leads the hungry heart in its quest for truth. Experiences are like open doors through which we pass. (No experience is finality.) As we pass through the doors, ever mindful of His ultimate intention, *we must surrender to the purpose of each crisis.*

Thus, while we are potential heirs by birth, there is much the Father cannot share until we are mature enough to appropriate. He waits to share the fuller measure of His light and love; but first our small capacity must be enlarged. He longs to share His peace and joy; but certain lessons must first be learned in His schoolroom. He waits to impart His wisdom and knowledge but only experience can make us partakers of this.

Finally, THRONESHIP: Romans 8:17 speaks of the glory which shall come after suffering. "If we suffer, we shall also reign with him..." (2 Tim. 2:12). It is not just suffering, but the suffering which results from learning obedience—that qualifies for the throne. There is even more involved in this qualifying for the throne which can be more fully appreciated as other truths unfold in the coming lessons.

Let us only say now, God's first call to man was to rulership over the earth (as he would qualify), and His last call to him is throneship with Him above the highest heaven. To enter into such joint-throneship with the Lord Jesus is almost beyond our comprehension. But as we shall see, this is the intention of the Father for those who qualify.

Finally, we can be sure man will never live beyond his vision. If mere salvation, victory, or restoration to paradise is the goal, reaching Romans eight is the ultimate. And the three phases of growth we have been considering will have little meaning. Yet once we come to God's larger outlook, and fully embrace *His Ultimate Intention,* we shall find a new throbbing in our breast—we shall discover what it means to be a God-centered son who lives with the ultimate in view.

10

WE ARE appreciating more and more how our starting point must always be THE FATHER: His desire, purpose and intention — for this is the only way we can keep proper perspective. It is the only way we can understand this important law of His working: All that He asks is wholly impossible to accomplish by natural strength and can only be realized by the resources He provides. This is His way of shutting men up to constant, utter dependence upon Him. It is what has often been termed . . .

The Call to Impossible Living

"IT IS NOT HARD to live the Christian life—it is impossible!" These words of Griffith Thomas are, oh, so true; because God has called us to *live by the life of Another*. The life He intends and the calling He has given can be realized only in His way and by His resources.

Adam faced this impossible calling as he stood at the gateway of choice. There were two ways open before him, as represented by two trees. Everyone since Adam has likewise had to learn that God will not yield *His* resources until men have laid down all that is natural.

There is no neutral ground. Man will either feed upon the tree of knowledge in accomplishing his own pursuits; or, as God has designed, he will come into union with Him, the Tree of Life, and receive God's boundless resources for realizing His intention. The grasping philosophy of life cannot be combined with the divine life of giving.

TWO WAYS – TWO PHILOSOPHIES

In the very midst of the garden was the tree of life, which seemed to occupy the most commanding position. There was no prohibition concerning its fruit. In its central place it represented the source of all growth and activity; and its name should have spoken to Adam, but he was slow to understand.

While he hesitated, his wife with Satan's help turned to another tree, the fruit of which God had distinctly prohibited. This tree, called the knowledge of good and evil, represented a life of independence – the way of selfish ambition. As we have been saying, from the beginning it was God's intention that Adam and his family should make a *moral choice*.

You will observe on the blackboard, we have pictured the two trees quite differently: the tree of life with its branches reaching heavenward illustrates the *way of giving*—the life dedicated unto God. The man who partakes of this manner of life is fulfilling the intention of God. He embraces heaven's way of life—the inwrought Cross. Because this life is reaching ever Godward, it is open to participation in full-heirship which means recovering the necessary resources as represented by the fruit of the tree.

We have pictured the other tree with its branches as they bowed down to entice Eve to a *way of grasping*. She was led to believe there was something in that tree *for her*. She acted independently of God and invited her husband to do the same. Together they were saying in effect: "Now we shall be as gods who can act in our own right. Of ourselves we will know what is good and what is evil." And in a sense it was true; they were becoming as little gods seeking complete freedom of action.

So when Adam and Eve took of the forbidden fruit, a new idea of independence developed in the mind of man. Watchman Nee explains this: "The emotion was touched, because the fruit was pleasant to the eyes, making him desire; the mind with its reasoning powers was developed for he was made wise; and the will was strengthened so that in the future he could always decide which way he would go." No longer utterly dependent upon God for instruction, man in his own eyes became independent.

LIVING BY THE SOUL, OR BY THE SPIRIT

Now that we understand the course which Adam took, we can see

LIVING — By Which Tree

GOD'S GOAL

ADAM

THE WAY OF GIVING — UNTO → IN DEPENDENCE UPON GOD HE SHARES

THE WAY OF GRASPING — FOR → BY INDEPENDENCE MAN FAILS

MAN'S PRIVATE GOAL

how this determined the lines of his development. It was God's intention that Adam should come into life-union with Himself. That is, the human spirit would come under the direction and government of the Holy Spirit by the birth-union. Adam's soul-faculties—the mind, emotions and will would then be used by the Spirit. However, when Adam chose to act independently by eating of the fruit of the tree of knowledge, he was ministering to the expansion and development of his soul-powers. Thereafter "man was not only a living soul, but from henceforth man would *live by the soul*" (Watchman Nee).

In brief, this meant that the human spirit, which had been God's avenue of contact with man, was no longer responsive. God had said, ". . . in the day that thou eatest thereof, thou shalt surely die." Thus sin not only separated man from God, but it alienated him from the very One who would have shared divine life with the human spirit. So man's spirit became dead toward God, instead of becoming spiritually and vitally united with Him as God intended.

The scientific definition of death helps us to understand what this means. Death is a falling out of correspondence with environment. By disobedience Adam turned away from his spiritual orientation. As the eye is dead when it no longer responds to the objects placed before it, or the ear is dead when it no longer responds to waves of sound, so man's spirit is dead (toward God) when it is unresponsive to Him.

So it is a matter of either living *by the soul* or *by the Spirit*. We must make this distinction, however. While God created Adam and gave him a soul, He did not intend for his spirit to become dead and thus necessitate his living *by the soul*. He did not intend for the soul to take the place of the spirit as the animating power of man. God so designed man that he must always possess a soul, but it is to be subservient to and become the instrument or vehicle through which the spirit expresses itself. Thus God's work of redemption is to set man's inner mechanism in right order, so that instead of living by the soul-powers, man comes into a spiritual union with God and begins to live by the Spirit. Thus God achieves His intention of "sonship"—the expression of His life in human beings.

It is just this simple: when we change the purpose and philosophy of life, we have changed trees. Christ who becomes our life will not allow us to pursue divine purposes in our own power. We are not called to production, but to participation in His life and pursuits. Israel learned this lesson through forty years of wandering in the wilderness. When God had called them to move into Canaan they saw the walled cities and the giants. The move was impossible in their natural strength.

Yet the walls of Jericho were just as thick and just as high forty years later. It was still impossible for natural strength or wisdom to devise the method that God finally indicated for taking the city. What was impossible became *Him-possible* by simple obedience and trust. While Israel's participation in God's method made them look ridiculous to the people inside the city, it was nevertheless the way she learned the secret of *impossible living*. We have been waiting until now to say there is no participating, appropriating or qualifying until we have learned to live from this Tree: HIM.

THE EXCHANGED LIFE

Recently I learned that the word "renew" in Isaiah 40:30 really means "exchange." Thus the text could correctly read, "But they that wait upon the Lord shall *exchange* their strength." This is the secret! The Christian exchanges his old manner of life and resources for the new. Weakness is exchanged for strength.

I suppose (says A. W. Tozer), it is improper to say that God makes His people strong, but we must understand this to mean that they become strong in exact proportion to their weakness; the weakness being their own and the strength being God's. "When I am weak then I am strong" is the way Paul said it, and in so saying set a pattern for every believer. What has happened is that he has switched from his little human battery to the infinite power of God.

Now remember we are still considering God's plan for our participation, appropriation and qualifying. This was God's first plan which has in no sense been changed by sin or the Fall. In the following lessons we will consider how redemption is incorporated into God's plan and we shall see that men have become so engrossed in the wonders of salvation they have missed the larger intention of God for His sons.

We are called not merely to receive His life, imparted by the new birth; we are called to a full participation in the life of Christ. We are called not merely to enjoy the bud, but to allow full blossoming of the flower. Let no one who is still allowing the selfish purpose of life to dominate, imagine that he is to any measure participating in this divine life. Jesus Christ will only live one kind of life in us: a life poured out unto the Father and for others. It is the snare of this present hour that men seem to want a crisis-impartation of His life *for themselves* but have little interest in daily manifesting His life unto God. We shall see how God designs this to be done as we consider . . .

THE METHOD OF APPROPRIATION

Surely it is this which stimulates the Apostle Peter to write, "According as his divine power hath given unto us all things that pertain unto life and godliness . . . and beside this, giving all diligence, add to your faith virtue . . ." (2 Pet. 1: 3, 5). Temptations, walls and giants are all a part of God's working. The Father does not provide for His sons the full maturity of the divine nature to be taken like milk from a bottle. When temptation to evil arises, Peter says, "Add to your faith virtue." When walls are too high, he says, "Add to virtue knowledge." The God who promised has a way. Learn it. Is the land filled with temporal blessing? Don't indulge. "Add to knowledge temperance." Do giants persist in the strongholds of Canaan? "Add patience." Do pagans invade your home with glittering false gods? Cast them out. There is a time for patience, but now "add godliness." Do neighbors and even brethren misunderstand and impose? "Add brotherly kindness" and love which means long suffering. When we have discovered that these cannot be appropriated from the *old tree*, we can see what has been our problem. It does make a difference. By which tree do we live — the natural or the spiritual?

Until we have truly been cut loose from the old tree, which is wild by nature, and grafted into the good tree; we have not learned to live from OUR NEW SOURCE. It is not by another trip to the altar, but by learning how to cooperate and appropriate that we "put on Christ."

Now, before we consider God's method of qualifying for the throne, let us be sure we have learned this law: with men (who rely on their natural resources) these things are impossible, but for those who are in union with God all things are possible—HIM-possible.

MARRIED TO ANOTHER

Hence it follows that shrinking from the way of the Cross, and our fainting on that way, even when we have begun to tread it, arises from ignorance of the blessedness to which the pathway leads. The most joyous moment in the life of the bride ought to be the moment when she loses her own name and self-dependence at the marriage-altar.

Taking her husband's name instead of her own, she loses her life in his. She is married to another and in this union has a new source of life. Likewise the most blissful moment of our life ought to be that in which we, by the work of the Cross, have renounced our right to self-ownership, and have reckoned ourselves dead to self, to sin and to the world, but gloriously alive *unto Him*. How well these lines by John Gregory Mantle describe this new *life union*.

> Oh, sacred union with the Perfect Mind,
> Transcendent bliss, which Thou alone canst give;
> How blest are they this Pearl of Price who find,
> And, dead to earth, have learned in Thee to live.

> Thus in Thine arms of love, O God, I lie,
> Lost, and for ever lost to all but Thee.
> My happy soul, since it hath learned to die,
> Hath found new life in Thine Infinity.

> Go then, and learn this lesson of the Cross,
> And tread the way that saints and prophets trod:
> Who, counting life and self and all things loss,
> Have found in inward death the life of God.

11

WE ARE continuing (as we shall throughout the book) to be centered in His viewpoint. What a fountainhead experience this is! To live at the very SOURCE of all things—the Father-heart! Until we arrive at this Paternal viewpoint we never quite realize just how much we were living with a "salvation complex" as though God's chief purpose and intention centered in Calvary and in the plan of salvation. Surely the Cross is central in God's plan of redemption and we would never minimize it. But now as we see the over-all Paternal purpose, we see beyond the Cross to the Father's ultimate intention for His Son — this becomes central and determines all else. But lest any should think we are overlooking the Fall and man's awful rebellion against God, let us see how the Father dealt with Satan and man the sinner, and understand how . . .

Redemption is Incorporated

MORE THAN EIGHT YEARS AGO we had a manuscript ready for the printers; but, because some of the material (at that time) seemed almost revolutionary in fundamental circles, we held up its publication. You can imagine what a joy it was to discover that a recent book, *The Normal Christian Life*, had been published in which Watchman Nee considered exactly those same aspects of truth which we are now to present. Let this be an encouragement to all. God's truth will go forth either through one channel or another. There is, of course, the proper time to plant His truth in His prepared seedbed.

With Watchman Nee we have repeatedly said:

Redemption is big enough, wonderful enough, to occupy a very large place in our vision; but God is saying that we should not make redemption to be everything, as though man were created to be redeemed. The Fall is indeed a tragic dip downwards in that line of purpose, and the atonement a blessed recovery whereby our sins are blotted out and we are restored; but when it is accomplished there yet remains a work to be done to bring us into possession of that which Adam never possessed, and to give God that which His heart desires. For God has never forsaken the purpose which is represented by that straight line.

Believers are prone to allow God's *recovery work* to overshadow His *realizing work*. We absolutely must see both in their proper place. Because of man's perverted tendencies toward self-relating, he has been more alive to *what God does for him*, than to *what he is destined to be unto God*. Our present lesson brings both aspects of God's work into view: (1) Through the Cross the work of the devil was destroyed; redemption and release from the bondage of sin and the effects of the Fall were provided, and: (2) Through the Cross provision was made whereby man can once again live to realize the Father's ultimate intention.

On the blackboard we have pictured X to Y: *the way of redemption through the Cross*, and Y to Z *the highway of realization through HIM*. Let us consider how the Blood and the Cross are two aspects which are remedial. First, in this lesson we see that God deals by the Blood with *all* that Adam *has done*. In the next lesson we see that He deals by the Cross with all that Adam *is* in his fallen state.

WHAT THE BLOOD MEANS TO GOD

It is a very wonderful day when we discover what the Blood means to God and in what sphere He intends for it to operate. In the Old Testament we have two very definite pictures which demonstrate how the Blood is primarily for God. If we would know the value God places upon it we must accept His Word regarding it:

First, consider the Passover in Egypt as described in Exodus 12:3-13. According to commandment the blood was put on the lintel and on the door posts. The meat of the lamb was to be eaten inside the house. God said, *"When I see the blood,* I will pass over you." It is clear that this blood was not meant to be presented to man to be seen, felt or understood by him. It· was wholly for the Lord. As an act

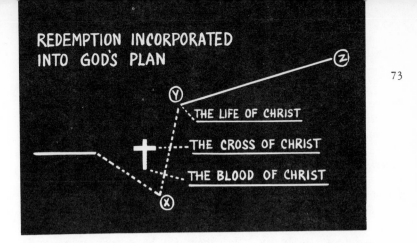

REDEMPTION INCORPORATED INTO GOD'S PLAN

THE LIFE OF CHRIST

THE CROSS OF CHRIST

THE BLOOD OF CHRIST

of faith and obedience they were to apply it to the door posts. All who were in the house could safely trust, because the blood would mean to God exactly what He said it would mean. It was not necessary for them to understand more. The sign of the blood on the door was GOD'S. By faith they rested in His satisfaction.

Second, the Day of Atonement, Leviticus 16, teaches us more. On this important day the sin offering for Israel was made publicly in the court of the tabernacle. The sacrifice was in full view of the people. But the blood of the sacrifice was taken into the most holy place, to be sprinkled before the Lord seven times by the high priest. This, too, was a transaction taking place between the high priest and God, away from the eyes of the people who were to benefit by it. The procedure from beginning to end was designed by God. The high priest, a type of the Lord Jesus, in obedience to God made an atonement. The people believed this act would mean to God exactly what He said.

From these two observances we understand that blood was offered in response to God's command. It was not for the human mind to grasp the significance or the human heart to feel what it meant. Man must simply obey and believe God's promise concerning it. Individuals are often stricken with what seems to be incurable guilt over some sin that looms larger in their vision than the Blood of Christ. "The whole trouble with these is that they are trying to sense it; trying to feel the value and to estimate subjectively what the Blood is for us. We cannot do it; it does not work that way. The Blood is first for God to see. We then have to accept God's valuation of it." (Watchman Nee).

This returns us to the point of God's sovereignty. Until we accept His Word and purpose unquestioningly, we will surely suffer confusion and misgiving. He cannot make His revelation clear as long as there is a point of controversy—a demand for further evidence which may be seen or felt. God must have the right to rule and govern the believer's life according to His own terms. Unquestioning faith in His promise concerning atonement and obedience to known truth precedes clear understanding of future steps.

Man is prone to try short-cuts which leave him stranded and questioning. God brings the prodigal back to the divine order only when he returns to cry, "I have sinned against Thee." Standing guilty, condemned in his conscience, the prodigal needs more than a *better feeling* about what he has done. He needs forgiveness for what he has done. The Blood is revealed to the penitent soul as legal grounds for forgiveness. He doesn't need to know how or why. He accepts what the Bible says concerning Jesus, "In whom we have redemption through his blood, the forgiveness of sins" (Ephesians 1:7, Colossians 1:14).

BOTH A CRISIS AND CONTINUAL CLEANSING

Since the Blood wholly satisfies the righteous requirements of God, the believer says, "Amen." The crisis of "being justified by His blood" (Romans 5:9) is like entering the gate. "Having therefore... boldness to enter into the holy place... let us draw near" (Hebrews 10:19, 22). We are not saved on one basis to maintain fellowship on another. The Blood provides continual cleansing. "If we walk in the light as he is in the light, we have fellowship one with another, and the blood of Jesus Christ his Son cleanseth us from all sin" (1 John 1:7).

This crisis experience occurs when we "who sometimes were far off are made nigh by the blood of Christ." In order that we may live with Him in the most holy place, we require daily cleansing. This is the secret of maintaining a God-centered position and His heavenly vantage point.

NOT A CLEANSED HEART, BUT A *NEW* ONE!

This may surprise you. But, did you know it is not really Scriptural to speak of "hearts being cleansed by the Blood?" This has been taught so long and so faithfully, it may be a jolt to realize the idea comes from a shallow interpretation of Hebrews 10:22. "Let us draw near with a true heart in full assurance of faith, *having our hearts sprinkled from an evil conscience*, and our bodies washed with pure water."

As one who has held for many years that this teaching attempts to make the Blood do something it was never intended to do, I was encouraged to find that Watchman Nee deals very positively with the question:

It may show a misunderstanding of the sphere in which the Blood operates to pray, "Lord, cleanse my heart from sin by Thy Blood!" The heart, God says, is desperately sick (Jeremiah 17:9), and He must do something more fundamental than cleanse it: He must give us a new one!

We do not wash and iron clothing that we are going to throw away. As we shall shortly see, the "flesh" is never to be cleansed; it must be crucified. The work of God within us must be something wholly new. "A new heart also will I give you, and a new spirit will I put within you" (Ezekiel 36:26).

There is a difference in seeing the Blood as a cleansing agent and as a legal satisfaction to God. The Blood is not intended to deal with sin in a subjective way. Its efficacy is objective, to be seen by God on the door post of the heart. The Hebrews passage concerning the work of the Blood does make reference to the heart, but it is actually in relation to the conscience. "Having our hearts sprinkled from an evil conscience," signifies something other than cleansing of the heart. It means something comes between God and myself, causing me to have an evil conscience whenever I seek to approach Him. The prick of my conscience is a constant reminder of the barrier of sin. But I see in God's Word that Jesus' Blood was shed for my forgiveness. When I trust and accept what the Blood means to Him, my conscience is cleared and this sense of guilt is removed.

Many have tried to cleanse away the old nature, the flesh, or the impurity of life. But death, not cleansing, is His answer to fallen man. God puts the whole of the old man in the grave. How blessed to see confused believers who once testified that the *Blood* had cleansed and made them pure, finally set free by the truth of death on the Cross. Others have never found the way of death by the Cross, and have fallen into disappointment and confusion, because the old man refused to be clean. God's only remedy for him is *death*.

God does not ask us to have faith in something that will not work. We cannot long convince ourselves that the Blood has cleansed when the old man continues to assert his unclean passions. But our faith can rest securely in the fact that God has accepted the sprinkling of Blood; our conscience is clear; we have been washed in the pure water of the Word. As "we are living and walking in the Light as He [Himself] is in the Light, we have fellowship . . . and the blood of Jesus Christ His Son (continually) cleanses (our conscience) us from all sin and guilt" (1 John 1:7 A.N.T.). (Words in parenthesis mine.)

THE MORE WE become accustomed to seeing from His viewpoint and thinking after His thoughts, the more we want to emphasize what God realizes for Himself through the Cross. Once we saw the Blood as it meant forgiveness for us. But now we see more — it is the ground on which the Father can enjoy fellowship with His children. Once we saw our union in Christ's death and resurrection as the basis for our victory; now we want to emphasize . . .

What the Cross Realizes for God

IN THE FIRST eight chapters of Romans, two aspects of salvation are presented: justification by the Blood and deliverance through the Cross. This is a most important distinction; for, alas, many believers have wandered in defeat for many years because they do not know or reckon on union in death with Christ on the Cross.

While we must be careful to recognize that Christ's finished work at Calvary is one complete work from God's standpoint, yet it is finished in the individual believer only as he reckons on its efficacy and allows the truth to become operative in his life. Let us see how this works.

IN ADAM . . . IN CHRIST

God deals with the human race through two representative men — Adam and Christ. A simple illustration will demonstrate the principle involved. By planting one kernel of corn, harvesting every kernel, and replanting year after year without destroying or using any of the corn; it would be possible to produce so much corn within twenty years that there would be no room for human life on the earth. Every grain of corn would have its beginning in the first tiny kernel.

This is what Paul speaks of in Romans 5:12-21 when he explains that we all had our beginning in the first Adam. Through him sin and death have come upon the human race. But through Christ comes the new creation wherein is righteousness – His righteousness.

Another illustration of this truth is found in Hebrews where the writer shows how Levi was in Abraham's loins when he paid tithes to Melchisedec. As the father of a family, Abraham is seen to include the whole family in himself. In making his offering he included with himself all his seed.

So it is that God sees two family trees: Adam's family and Christ's family. If our source of life is to change it becomes evident that above all, one thing must happen. We must change families. Since we are born into Adam's family, how can we get out? How can we become disentangled from the wretchedness of our inheritance through him? There is only one way to be freed. That is through death. By union with Christ (the last Adam) in His death, God sets us free from the tyrants who reign over Adam and his posterity.

God not only speaks of the *first* and *last* Adam, but also of the *first* and *second* man. The realization that there would never be another Adam brought to me a wonderful unveiling of truth. When the Lord Jesus was crucified on the Cross, He was nailed there and laid in the tomb as the "last Adam." All that was in the first Adam was gathered up and done away in Him. In God's reckoning, Adam was left in the grave. We were included there.

By Jesus' death the old race was completely wiped out. Do you see it? There will never be another Adam. As Christ, "the last Adam," moved into death, He carried the whole family into the grave and God pronounced: THE END! But in the "second Man," He brings forth the new race by the resurrection.

"The first man is of the earth earthy: the second man is the Lord from heaven.... And as we have borne the image of the earthy, we shall also bear the image of the heavenly..." (1 Cor. 15:47-49). Now by one master stroke God has provided death to the old and the earthy; but He has provided life through the second Man, the Lord Jesus, who becomes the life-source of the new, heavenly creation. Through death, burial and resurrection we pass from the old family tree into a new family tree. We are no longer "in Adam" but are now "in Christ."

In this new position God considers us beyond the claims of old tyrants and under His new government. What God counts as true of our position, we must appropriate as true in our life and walk. What a day it is when we recognize all that He designed to accomplish through the Cross. In it God has liberated Adam's race from four reigning tyrants; death, sin, the law, and the flesh. Paul gives us this birds-eye view in the middle chapters of Romans:

Chapter 5, freedom from sin's penalty – death.

Chapter 6, freedom from sin's tyranny – bondage.

Chapter 7, freedom from sin's strength – the law.

Chapter 8, freedom from sin's presence – when we receive the redemption of the body.

Paul emphasizes that being moved positionally from Adam into Christ is more, much more than having a new family position. In Adam we receive all that was of Adam as the life-source. Now, in Christ, we are to receive everything that is of Christ—our new Life-source. God intends this new life to be more than a position or a crisis experience. It is to be a new way of living—a new purpose for existence. Thank God, the hour has come when He is making His manner and purpose of life effectual in more of His children than ever before. But just here men so often take a detour and miss THE KEY which will surely open the way of life unto God.

THE IMPORTANT KEY

Many times in the past fifteen years of ministering in Bible conferences, folk have confessed to me, "We have tried to make the truth of identification with Christ in death and resurrection real in our lives. Yet in spite of all our knowing, reckoning and yielding, it hasn't seemed to bring reality. It has not brought the victory and blessing which we sought."

As I listen the problem becomes evident. Their very words reveal it. Without realizing the truth, these people are far more concerned for themselves than for Him. They are far more alive to what they want God to do *for them,* than what they might become *unto Him.* If they could, they would use God and the work of the Cross for their own ends. Here is the source of their trouble! The Cross is not the threshold to selfish attainment, but a terminal to selfishness. Many would use it for themselves, but God has designed that it should bring men wholly unto Himself.

Even among those who continually attend deeper life conferences and retreats, we find many who have fallen victim of this vicious snare. After years and years of reckoning on more knowledge and deeper teaching they are still camping around their old self-center: getting all God has *for me*, possessing all *my possessions*, appropriating all *my inheritance* in Christ.

Oh! May God shatter the veneer and uncover every attempt at *using* the Cross, instead of *dying on* the Cross. Hidden behind most begging and pleading for God to give victory is the secret concern for ourselves—not Himself. God will not condone this self-centeredness. How many years I taught the truths of Romans six and counseled with those who were in defeat and bondage before I found this key—In His death I am to become *alive unto God!* As long as a believer's primary concern is to get victory or deliverance it means, that in a subtle way, he continues to live unto self. Four times in four verses in Romans six God emphasizes that the key is *living unto God:*

Vs 10 —"... liveth unto God."

Vs 11 —"... alive unto God."

Vs 13 —"... yield yourselves unto God."

Vs 13 —"... as instruments unto God."

What does God intend this to mean in actual practice? Simply that the primary thing He will realize through the Cross is to change man's old center and purpose of living and bring him unto Himself and His ultimate intention. Here is the ancient law—when we seek Him first, then all these things will be added. The very moment one becomes alive unto God the door has opened for Him to accomplish victory and full deliverance.

TWO FAMILIES AND TWO TREES

On the blackboard we have pictured the two families and their corresponding trees. One is the family "in Adam" and the other is the family "in Christ." All who have their source in the life of Adam have followed in his selfish way by living unto their own purpose and plans. Now through the Cross, God has laid the axe to the root of the old family tree, in order that He might move man into a new family, and *life unto God.* Such a life is from a new source.

One glance at our modern emphasis would teach us that Satan's methods have not changed one whit since the Garden. He is still offering the same substitute for the tree of life. Today it is a modern cross in place of the old rugged Cross. In an earlier book (now out of

THE WORK of the CROSS IN CHRIST

IN ADAM

LIFE
RIGHTEOUSNESS
LOVE
SPIRIT

DEATH
SIN
LAW
FLESH

print) we quoted A. W. Tozer:

The new cross says "Come and get." And a selfish human would be entirely contrary to his own nature if he refused. Of course he will use the Cross for his own benefits. Whereas the old rugged Cross says, "Come and give," and for the moment entirely ignores anything that the individual shall receive, save a baptism into death. And why does the old Cross demand so much? Simply because from the beginning God has only intended that this Christian life shall be based on this one principle: The new life is lived not unto self but unto God. (2 Cor. 5:14).

Whereas the old Cross was meant by God to be the symbol of death and detachment from the old Adam life, this new substitute cross does not intend to slay the sinner but just redirect him. It gears him into a cleaner, jollier way of living and saves his self-center and ambition. To the self-assertive it says: "Come and assert yourself for Christ." To the religious egotist it says: "Come and do your boasting in the Lord." To the thrill seeker it says: "Come and enjoy the thrill of Christian fellowship." The modern message is slanted in the direction of the current vogue, thereby catering to human taste and reasoning.

The old Cross would have no truck with the world. For Adam's proud flesh it meant the end of the journey. It carried into effect the sentence imposed by the law of Sinai. The new cross is not opposed to the human race, rather it is a friendly pal, and if understood aright, it is the source of oceans of good clean fun and innocent enjoyment. It lets Adam live without interference. His life motivation is unchanged; he still lives for his own pleasure, only now he takes delight in singing choruses and watching religious movies instead of singing bawdy songs and drinking hard liquor. The accent is still on enjoyment, though the fun is now on a higher plane morally, if not intellectually.

If this was true fifteen years ago when it was first written, how much more it is true today. One need only watch the converts of this "new cross" to realize that they have never had a changed center through union with Jesus in death on the old rugged Cross. But what is more alarming is that even our deeper life conferences have become victims (unconsciously, I trust) of this new philosophy and technique. To be sure the "new cross" approach has become popular because it has slipped in all unannounced and undetected. On the surface it appears to use the vocabulary of the old rugged Cross. Yet the likenesses are superficial while the differences are fundamental. The "new cross" offers a living unto self. The old Cross points to the heavenly way of living unto God.

THE HOLY SPIRIT MUST REVEAL

I shall never forget one Sunday night several years ago when we were speaking about these two family trees. In using the blackboard I had spoken from Romans 11 using God's description of how the Gentiles of the wild olive tree were grafted into the good olive tree so that they might become partakers of new life from the good tree. Of course I showed how this portion of Scripture directly applied to God's cutting Israel off and grafting in the Gentiles; yet I showed how the principle applies to God's cutting us off from the old family of Adam and, through death, moving us into Christ. In Him we have a new root, and if the root is holy, so are the branches.

How often the Holy Spirit accomplishes more in one instant of revelation than in years of preaching or teaching. It was so that night. Suddenly the dear pastor's wife stood to her feet and walked to the front. Tears coursed down her cheeks as she told how God had been speaking to her for days about living from the source and in the bondage of the old Adam life.

Then she explained, "God could never have spoken more directly to me about my wild-olive living." Turning to me she said, "Others knew, but you didn't. My first name is Olive. And these people know all too well how much of my life has been from the source of the old, wild Olive." During five weeks of ministry in that church the Holy Spirit graciously liberated many who had been living from the "old family tree." Now by a real union in death and resurrection they moved into a "new family" and purposeful living unto God.

In God's planning then, the Cross and the crucified One have become the gateway to LIFE. Apart from this gateway there can be no movement on the highway of realizing God's purpose. While we are not unmindful of the pit from whence we have been digged, nor the Rock to which we have come, we do not linger in preoccupation with these. We move ever forward to realize the purpose for which we have been called to sonship. We shall always sing about the precious Blood, glory in the Cross, and exult in His life, but what previously have been crises will now become a walk forward and upward in fulfilling His ultimate intention. This is truly life—a new kind of life in a wholly different sphere. Death has yielded its throne to the higher law of love; the flesh has yielded its throne to the Spirit. All this is what the Cross has realized for God.

13

FROM THE Paternal outlook we realize that it was the Father's purpose "before the foundation of the world" that men should share His life. It was not because man sinned, but even before he sinned, that God determined "in the fulness of time" to share life through His Son. Had Adam obeyed God and thus been enlightened to see the value of the tree of life, he could have entered into sonship. Then by a constant eating of this tree (which represented Christ) he could have moved along the Highway of Realizing God's ultimate intention. Now in spite of Adam's fall, God has made provision that Christ might become the continuing tree of life. It is simply a fulfilling of God's original design for man . . .

To Live by the Life of Another

AT LAST WE HAVE ARRIVED at the highway where man can begin to realize God's ultimate intention. You will observe that God has lifted fallen man up to resurrection life (see "1" on blackboard). We have been making the distinction between the "way up"—which involves God's work of redemption, and the "highway on" which means the life of realization for God.

Too many have never understood that God uses the Blood and the Cross in a remedial way by which He intends to bring us unto life. By the Cross He has been cutting us loose from our old natural resources that we might live by the life of Another. Of course from God's standpoint, man has had divine life from the initial moment he was born-from above. But just as God revealed the value of the Blood to reconcile and forgive, or the value of our union in death with Christ for our deliverance, even so it must come as a revelation that we are cut off from the old source of natural life. Now we are to live and move by the life-resources of Another.

I must frankly admit that for more than ten years I had been occupied in my ministering with the aspects of the Cross that deal with sin and its power. Then the revelation dawned! I was like a branch that had been detached—now I must become attached—grafted to Him, the *trunk of life*. Not only are we united with Him in the likeness of His death, but also in His resurrection. I saw why Paul in Romans 5:10 was urging them to recognize still another "much more." "... being reconciled to God by the death of His Son, MUCH MORE... we shall be saved [daily delivered from sin's dominion] through His resurrection life." (A.N.T.)

Just as we must not separate Christ's death *for sin* from the believer's death with Christ *to sin*, neither should we separate that union in death from union in resurrection life. The Christian life is not a *changed life. It is an exchanged life!* "I live, and yet no longer I, but Christ liveth in me" (Gal. 2:20). This life is not something we ourselves can produce. It is actually *living by the life of Another*.

In the second chapter of Ephesians we note three aspects which describe our living this new life:
1. a resurrection life (verse 1)
2. a reigning life (verse 6)
3. a realizing life (verse 10)

Shall we look first at the nature of this new resurrection life: Paul says, "And you hath he quickened (made alive) who were dead..." (vs. 1). Once we were dead to God and alive only to the mind of the

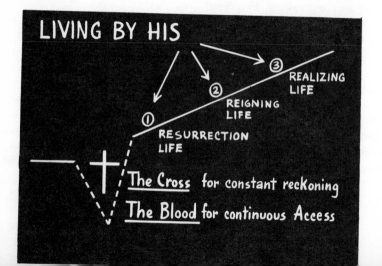

flesh and the cravings after this world. Now, through union in death and resurrection we receive a new mind—His mind. As we have said before, this is truly entering Romans 8. Instead of being ruled by a carnal mind which works death, we now have a spiritual mind, which means life and peace.

Furthermore when we learn how the sentence of death rests upon the body of flesh, we can cease to walk after the pull of the body; thus we experience the operation of the Spirit who quickens our mortal body. Let no one minimize God's quickening work. Too little is known and experienced of living in HIS RESURRECTION LIFE.

Many years ago I remember hearing how A. B. Simpson, founder of The Christian and Missionary Alliance, learned to live by the life of Another. According to his own testimony "once he sought for healing" as a crisis for his weakened body, but then he realized he was to enter into a union—living constantly by the strength of Another. He accomplished the work of many men through this LIFE-UNION.

One day when he was finishing a series of meetings, the pastor friend insisted that it would be wise for him to take some time for rest instead of going on to the next appointment. Some months later when the pastor discovered how God had used Mr. Simpson at that meeting, he asked him for the secret of his strength. Whereupon he simply said: "I have learned to live by the life of Another. That day as I rode on the train, each time the wheels turned about I just took in a deep breath, reminding myself I was actually absorbing HIS LIFE AND STRENGTH."

How many would like to use this formula! But it does not work that way. *He* does the using. Nor does one look back to some long ago crisis and say, "I understand what you are talking about, because I was filled with His power twenty years ago." What we are speaking of here is a continuous union with the living Christ. He is ever abiding in us and putting forth His mighty resurrection energy through us to fulfill the Father's intention. This life-union will only work in living unto Him. There is much more that could be said, but we must now pass on to examine:

THE REIGNING LIFE

First we need to be clear as to the object and scope of this reigning life. We are not only quickened (with resurrection life), but we are (vs. 6) "raised up together and made to sit together in heavenly places in Christ Jesus." It becomes clear that this life also possesses authority over principalities and powers of darkness. A few verses earlier we read (Eph. 1:20-22) that God "raised Him (Christ) from the dead, and set Him at His own right hand... far above all principality, and power, and might, dominion, and... hath put all things under His feet...."

Yes, God's original commission to man was that he should *have dominion* over the world in which he had been placed. This authority passed after the fall to Satan, who since that day has been the "prince of this world" under whose sway the whole race of mankind lies.

The Lord Jesus Christ at Calvary finally and forever broke the power of this empire of darkness. Just in the same way that the dominion of sin has been shattered for those in Christ, so also has Adam's lost empire been restored in Him.

Thus we come to another "much more" in Romans 5:17. Paul now says: "... much more they... shall reign in life by one, Jesus Christ." So it is not just a matter of having His resurrection life; but we are also to learn what it means to reign by His life.

There is something far deeper here than meets the casual eye. Satan's power lies not just in the love of the world, or sin, or in some direct assault on our mind or body. We may overcome all of these and yet live under the "sting and fear of death." Here is the real question: have we really faced the question of death? As long as we still ."love our life" we are still a victim of the enemy's last weapon: death. Where there is still the fear of death, we cannot say we have overcome him by — loving not our life unto the death. (Rev. 12:11).

His brother had just been poisoned because he was a Christian chief. The pagan tribe, with less than a dozen Christians, had learned by former experience that Christian chiefs — well, there were none like them.

"Have you considered taking the position as chief of this pagan tribe?" asked the missionary.

"Yes, I have prayed about it and I believe I should accept the position."

"But do you realize all the risk it involves? Your brother was poisoned just because he was a Christian."

"Yes, I know that, I do not know what day I may be poisoned, but what a great opportunity for serving these people."

Renouncing all that he had, even to life itself, the native Christian accepted the position of chief. Loving not his life (even unto death) was the means by which God would realize His ultimate through him. As it was with the Lord Jesus, so it is with those who stand identified in His "reigning life." Death has been robbed of its sting. But it goes even further. It means a willingness to lay down our life for others. This is reigning. Let the devil do his worst. We already stand in death. But we also stand in Life – in His REIGNING LIFE!

Next let us consider His REALIZING LIFE. This is creative life. We can be sure we are not going to advance one step on the highway of realizing God's intention until His resurrection and reigning life are operating through us in a *creative way.*

How few believers there are who have found God's plan for their lives. How few, who are abandoned to the purpose for which God has placed them in this world! We are largely playing at Christian work in these days. We go in and out of services and meetings. We like, perhaps, to preach, or are content to offer what we conceive to be some help to His work; and we give a little of our money to Christian causes which appeal to us. Yet we have missed the real issue; all Christian service must result in action, creative not imitative action.

Listen! "We are His workmanship, created in Christ Jesus UNTO GOOD WORKS, which God hath before ordained that we should walk in them" (Eph. 2:10). Here is what He has predestined you to be in Christ Jesus—a vessel through whom He will work creatively. This is not optional. We have said before, this divine life can only be manifest *unto God.* From the beginning God has marked out every son to fill a niche which no one else can fill. Just as surely as we live by His life, shall we recognize that ours is an ordered life—a God planned life.

What is His plan for you? How will He live and pour His life out through you? Is it to preach His name in the dark places of the earth? Is it faithfully to fill some humble office for which you are specially equipped in order that others may be released for the more prominent work? Is it to seek to train the young so they may go out into life with a solid foundation? Is it to bring up a family so that they in their turn may fit into that special place in His purpose? What is His plan for you? If you do not know, it is tantamount to a denial of His crown rights in your life. Remember! From the beginning—the very beginning you have been "created in Christ Jesus" unto a REALIZING LIFE.

With this we complete the first half of this book—13 chapters. Now we are ready to consider what it means to live unto His Ultimate Intention. We shall see all that is involved in walking on the HIGHWAY OF REALIZATION.

14

FINALLY WE HAVE COME to the lesson wherein God unveils His ULTIMATE INTENTION in the Cross. We realize as long as man is still interpreting the Cross as it benefits him, as it works for his own safety, security and victory, he is wearing a pair of colored glasses. He has missed that rectification which comes as man lives in the Paternal viewpoint, and philosophy. But as the believer begins to interpret the Cross as an eternal principle which God intends to be operative in him, then he sees the Cross in a new light—as it realizes for God. Instead of only appropriating the work of the Cross, this means he will embrace . . .

The Way of the Cross

THERE IS A BIG DIFFERENCE! First we learn to appropriate the *work of the Cross;* then as the Cross becomes inwrought in the believer —we learn the *way of the Cross.* Appropriating emphasizes what man receives. The Cross-principle inwrought emphasizes what the Father receives through His sons. The two aspects are not necessarily separate in experience but each must have its particular work in the life of the believer who presses on the highway living *unto God.*

We may speak of entering *the way of the Cross* when the Cross ceases to be only external; and when it becomes operative within the believer. Instead of the accent on man's receiving, it is on the Father's realizing HIS ULTIMATE INTENTION in the Cross.

Once this has come as a revelation, it will be evident that this phase has been almost overlooked. The writer of Hebrews must have had this in mind when he said, "Therefore leaving the principles of the doctrine of Christ, let us go on..." (Heb. 6:1). The Apostle Paul seems to insist that this *way of the Cross* is the evident reason that his own ministry is fruitful and effective:

"For we which live are always delivered unto death FOR JESUS' SAKE, that the life also of Jesus might be made manifest in us. So then death worketh in us... but life in you" (2 Cor. 4:11).

How strange this seems to those who are ever seeking *to get* and have not yet come alive to what God might receive through their lives. Of course they cannot appreciate or understand Paul's purpose of life. They have somehow missed the importance of one little phrase which Paul continually emphasizes. It is used in a similar context in his letter to the Romans:

We are daily accounted as sheep for the slaughter..."FOR THY SAKE" (Rom. 8:36).

We are daily delivered unto death "FOR JESUS' SAKE" (2 Cor. 4:11). Previously we saw everything "for our sake." But now as we move along this highway, it means interpreting this working of death as FOR JESUS' SAKE.

What a privilege and calling is ours! God has chosen and designed us to be transparent vessels to display heaven's treasure—vessels through which He might continually reveal to others the dying of the Lord Jesus. What seems to be "our dying" is really the "dying of the Lord Jesus" in us. This "working of death" becomes the means of life to all to whom it is revealed.

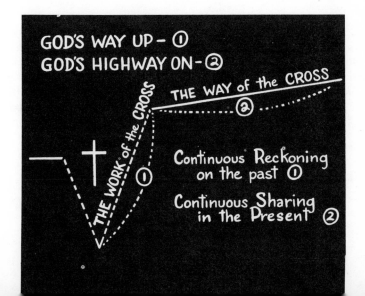

THE REASON FOR BARREN LIVING

Many of God's children approach the *way of the Cross* with be-wilderment and hesitancy. Not understanding what was in God's mind before the Fall, nor the heavenly philosophy of life, they shudder at the thought of a constant *working of death*. "I'm not ready for that pathway, I want abundant life and joy—not death."

A letter from a student in a Christian college discerns the spirit of modern Christendom. "Since I've been away from home and the fellow-ship, the issues have become much clearer. I see so many who are apparently dedicated to service but not to any sacrifice with it. At first I was bewildered. Maybe I was too narrow in choosing to give up my rights and allow the *working of death* as I had been taught. I saw the careless expenditure of God's money on extravagant things. I was tempted. But then the Lord allowed me to see how barren and empty these lives were. Those who seemed to reign as kings knew little of the *way of the Cross*."

DIVINE LIFE CANNOT BE USED

To move along the highway of realization and enjoy living by the life of Another is not the way of least resistance, even though you may be surrounded by Christians. A shock comes to those who find them-selves on *another highway* altogether, because the Christ-life can only be lived in one way—unto God and poured out for others. The moment we think we can settle down to use Him (His life) for our own living, He (His life) won't be ours to use. Divine life does not operate that way.

We have not been delivered from the world as long as we continue to interpret Calvary as it will benefit us. Even though we may share the "benefits" with those who are lost, we are doing so in our own way while preserving our own right to rule. Multitudes of believers are in captivity to a world system of *security* and *reward*. God waits to turn their captivity when they come to the end of their own ways. But He will never thrust His way upon anyone. It is our privilege and glad-hearted choice to move onto a highway where life is *unto Him*.

THE PAST AND PRESENT

In God's reckoning, the work of the Cross has been once for all finished. We should always make this distinction. When we reckon upon

Christ's death *for us* and our *death with Him,* we use the past tense, saying with Paul:

"I have been crucified..."

"Our old man was crucified..."

"Reckon yourselves... to be dead..."

In these and many other instances Paul pictures our union "together with Him." We are delivered from sin's guilt and its power by reckoning on our identification with the finished work of Christ on the Cross. There is a finality—we are to reckon on what is past.

There are some who confuse this with another of Paul's statements and assume we are called to "die daily" to sin. NO! Paul insists we are *dead to sin.* From the time of our first knowledge of Christ's redemptive work, and our appropriation by reckoning it ours, we have been dead to sin. In any dispute with Satan, or uprising of the flesh, we reckon from the time of our *first reckoning.* It is always past! Finished!

When Paul said, "I die daily," he was not saying that we are called to die daily to sin. It is just at this point many confuse the "work" of the Cross and the "way" of the Cross. The first is a past tense reality which we reckon upon. The latter is a present tense reality which we share with Christ continually.

Jesus, who as the last Adam entered the world sinless, needed only to embrace the *way* of the Cross. He said, "If any man would come after me, let him deny himself and take up his cross daily and follow me" (Luke 9:23). This is often misused to teach that by some measure of self-discipline man can put the old self to death by a daily denial. This is utterly frustrating to the grace of God! We must keep two aspects of truth in their proper place. Two different men are involved. The Lord Jesus identified Himself with the human race, enfolded us in Himself and took us to the tomb. Now God reckons that we are not only dead but buried. This was the end of the Adam race. Jesus was the last Adam. Now we are risen from the dead and alive in the Lord Jesus, who is also spoken of as the second Man. We with Him are a *new creation* — a completely *new man.*

NOTE THE DIFFERENCE

The *old man in Adam* experiences the *work* of the Cross. The *new man in Christ* is called to embrace the *way* of the Cross. We reckon our death to the old Adam, standing on Christ's finished work, always in the past tense. We now daily share in the new Man that divine *way* of life, which works death in us but *life* to others.

In another figure, we hand ourselves over to God, that as a kernel of wheat we may be planted in death in order to bring forth much fruit. Paul refers to this new man when he says "always bearing about in the body the dying of the Lord Jesus, that the life also of Jesus may be manifested in our body." It is faulty interpretation of the Scripture that leads us to assume that God would put heaven's treasure in anything but *a new man*.

Let us now consider more carefully four portions of Scripture, often confused with the old man, which actually apply to the new. It is the new man, who because of ministry stands "in jeopardy every hour." For this reason Paul says, "I die daily." The context is very plain. There is no reference to dying to sin. The Apostle speaks of his daily willingness to hazard his life for the gospel. The passage reads: "If the dead rise not... why stand we in jeopardy every hour?...I die daily. If by the manner of men I have fought with beasts at Ephesus, what advantageth it me, if the dead rise not?" (1 Cor. 15:30-32).

T. A. Hegre writes, "It would require the greatest stretch of the imagination and the greatest liberty in exegesis to apply this phrase, 'I die daily,' to death to sin. It does not at all refer to sin..., but to Paul's willingness to sacrifice his life that others might live."

Another passage often interpreted as having to do with death to sin is found in John 12:24. Jesus said, "Except a corn of wheat fall into the ground and die, it abideth alone: but if it die, it bringeth forth much fruit." Any farmer plants *good* seed—seed with life in it. Seed is planted not for purification but for production. We are as seed in His hand.

DEAD – BUT ALSO DYING

For many years I was puzzled about Paul's desire as expressed in Philippians 3:10. Six years before this writing he testified, "I have been crucified with Christ—[in Him] I have shared His crucifixion; it is no longer I who live, but Christ, the Messiah lives in me; and the life I now live in the body I live by faith—by adherence to *and* reliance on *and* [complete] trust—in the Son of God, Who loved me and gave Himself up for me" (Gal. 2:20 A.N.T.).

Why should one who testified to such a death later say, "That I may know him, and the power of his resurrection, and the fellowship of his sufferings, being made conformable unto his death; if by any means I might attain unto the resurrection of the dead?" (Phil. 3:10). If one is dead is he not dead? How then could Paul long to die again or continue to die?

It was not until I understood the distinction we have been making that I realized Paul was no longer speaking about the dying of the *old man*. He is speaking as God's *new man*—it is his purpose to "fill up that which is behind of the afflictions of Christ *in my flesh* for his body's sake, which is the church..." (Col. 1:24). As he shared more deeply in Christ's suffering by conforming to the way of the Cross, he would know greater resurrection power. We also have the same joy and privilege to be identified with the Lord Jesus in ministry.

In 2 Corinthians 1:8-9 (A.N.T.), another passage makes this truth clear: "For we do not want you to be uninformed brethren, about the affliction and oppressing distress which befell us in [the province of] Asia, how we were so utterly and unbearably weighted down and crushed that we despaired even of life [itself.] Indeed, we felt within ourselves that we had received the [very] sentence of death; but that was to keep us from trusting and depending on ourselves instead of on God Who raises the dead."

Conformity to death on the resurrection side of the Cross means a deepening weakness in ourselves, not an increasing sense of strength! Our natural desire is to feel we are strong and can do this or that. Weakness is the *way of the Cross*, for we live by the *life* and *strength* *of Another.*

Let us quote the testimony of Mrs. Penn-Lewis, who tells of a crisis in her life which came after her deliverance from the dominion of sin. While enjoying the *work of the Cross* as it meant a joyous experi-she began to read a volume on the Way of the Cross. She says:

As I read the book, I clearly saw the way of the Cross and all that it would mean. At first I flung the book away, and said, "No, I will not go that path. I shall lose all my glory experience." But the next day I picked it up again, and the Lord whispered so gently, "If you want deep life, and unbroken communion with God, this is the way." I thought, "Shall I? No!" And again I put the book away. The third day I again picked it up. Once more the Lord spoke, "If you want fruit, this is the path. I will not take the conscious joy from you, you may keep it if you like; but it is either that for yourself, or this and fruit. Which will you have?" And then, by His grace I said, "I choose the path for fruitfulness," and every bit of conscious experience closed. I walked for a time in such complete darkness—the darkness of faith, that it seemed almost as if God did not exist. And again, by His grace, I said, "Yes, I have only got what I agreed to," and on I went to take some meetings, and then I saw the fruit. From that hour I understood, and knew intelligently, that it was dying, not doing, that produced spiritual fruit. The secret of a fruitful life is—in brief —to pour out to others and want nothing for yourself: to leave yourself utterly in the hands of God and not care what happens to you. (From Memoirs by M.N. Garrard.)

One need only read the writings of men who knew much about the Cross, to realize how this matter of the Cross once-for-all and the "Cross-daily" has always seemed like a paradox. Bishop Moule calls it an "Inexhaustible paradox; on one side, a true and total self-denial, on the other, a daily need of crucifixion." Surely the answer lies, as we have been pointing out, in keeping these two phases distinct: the work of the Cross which deals with the old Adam-life, and the way of the Cross which the new man gladly embraces as a daily pathway.

Recall Jacob's midnight crisis when God put the sentence of death upon the strength of *old-Jacob*. Even when he came forth in his new name, Israel, God designed that he should bare the mark of lameness. It was to be a constant reminder that he was not to walk after the old life of the flesh, but in the strength of his new life: Israel. So it is as the *new man* in Christ that we learn our own weakness in ourselves, but that our constant source of strength is in Him. Mary N. Garrard pictures the new man, Israel, thus:

> "The lame shall take the prey."
> And I am lame--
> Lame in my inmost soul,
> Oh Saviour, make me whole!
> But ever keep me lame enough
> To be of use to Thee.

> If Thou shouldst make me strong--
> Strong in myself--
> To wrestle, fight and pray,
> Toil for Thee night and day,
> I might unwittingly soon cease
> To be wrecked upon Thee.

> So leave me with the lameness Jacob had
> Halting upon his thigh;
> That when, amid the battle sorely pres't,
> The victory of the Cross is manifest
> Through my prevailing prayer, the praise
> May be wholly to Thee.

For here is victory —
   Give me the power
To fight until the sword cleave to my hand,
And "having overthrown them all, to stand,"
And be content for only God to know
Who wrought with Him that day.

THE MORE WE understand from His viewpoint what is the ultimate intention in the Cross, the more we recognize how the Early Church invaded and conquered the known world in such a few years. If we marvel at what happened so quickly through them, we might be more amazed at what God could do in these last days. There was nothing so mysterious about those early believers; they were simply a living demonstration of . . .

The Cross in Three Dimensions

THE CROSS AS a *principle* is an expression of a divine way of life. The Cross as a *place* is where the divine and earthly ways of life come into conflict. The Cross as a *power* is the means by which God works through believers.

PRINCIPLE

Two boys, brought before a judge for throwing stones at a passenger train, seemed to show no sign of sorrow or repentance for their behavior. The older of the two sneered, "Judge, I'm only sorry we missed the windows."

Without explanation the judge drove the boys to his home, and took them to the basement where he showed them a complicated system of model trains. Their eyes grew wide with disbelief as he encouraged them to turn the switches and control the traffic on the tracks. They were cautious, but eager. Soon they were absorbed in the wonders of the tiny railroad. The judge looked on with satisfaction. His plan was going to work. When the moment for unveiling came, he turned to the boys and said, "Fellas, how would you like these trains? To move to your home, I mean. I've decided to give them to you, if you want them."

There was a long silence. Finally one of the boys with tears streaming down from his eyes sobbed, "But I don't understand. We've been so mean, . . . and now you're giving *these* to us? Why?" The other joined in, "Judge, we don't deserve anything so nice." They both broke; they wept; they pled with the judge to forgive them and promised they would never do such meanness again.

One of the boys, now a man, told the story. "That judge led us to Christ and became a spiritual father to us. If it hadn't been for his wisdom in dealing with two wayward boys, I would not be sitting at the bar as a Christian judge today." In this incident we see the Cross in three dimensions: As a principle, as a place and as a power.

PLACE

Through a juvenile judge who manifested the love and compassion of Christ in the face of hatred and enmity, the Father made His heart understandable to the warped and blinded minds of two boys. Self-will brought the youngsters into conflict with law. But the significant conflict was between unreasoned hate in the heart of the boys and unexplicable love in the heart of the judge. *At the juncture of human hate and divine love a cross always appears.* The Cross becomes a place.

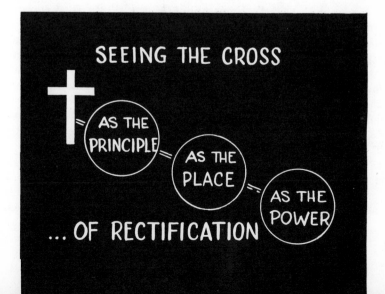

When the Lord Jesus, God's glorious Invader from above, came to bring a divine way, purpose and philosophy of life to this dark world, two opposing ways came into constant conflict. The way of *giving* always exposes the way of *getting*. The hour of supreme conflict had come. Satan understood the purpose of Christ's mission, and knew it would mean the eventual destruction of his kingdom. So the prince of this world, the arch-enemy of all that is true, set out to destroy and hinder Christ from the manger to the Cross.

Lesson eight showed how Christ dealt with the tempter in the wilderness. Three times in the temptation He affirmed heaven's way and philosophy of living. To respond to Satan's suggestions by doing anything *for* Himself, *of* Himself, or *with* Himself would have been out of harmony with His dedication to the Father. Though the devil offered Him the kingdoms of the world apart from the Cross, He could not be moved. Satan always opposes the Cross-principle. Christ always manifests it.

For more than three years while Christ lived among men, He was ever revealing their selfishness, exposing their self-seeking and uncovering their warped purpose in life. He left no one neutral. Either men must accept Him and His divine way of life, or they must find grounds to reject and dispose of Him.

And this is the lesson we must learn: He who embraces the Cross as an inwrought principle in his daily living will become a "cross"—a constant point of conflict—to reveal all who insist upon any other way and manner of life. Oh, the revealing and rectifying power of such a life!

POWER

One who embraces the Cross-principle and allows it to accomplish its full work by exposure and conflict is constantly energized by *divine power*. Thus the inwrought Cross becomes in God's hand a mighty demonstration of power. Such a demonstration in the lives of believers is more than a moral influence. Paul says, "The preaching (word) of the cross is to them that perish foolishness; but unto us which are saved it is the power of God" (1 Cor. 1:18).

Multitudes of God's people are praying for power, but few realize God's only reason for enduing His children with power is that they might give their lives for Him. Many have missed the real import of Acts 1:8: "But ye shall receive power after that the Holy Ghost is come upon you: and ye shall be witnesses unto me...." The word for witnesses is *martus* and means martyr. Too often our attention has been focused on power to do some bold exploit, to move multitudes, to become great deliverers. There will be exploits and multitudes will be moved, but the deeper truth is that we have a *divine energy* to "love not our lives even unto death." The words witness and martyr were once interchangeable because witnesses let no circumstance silence their full testimony concerning Jesus Christ.

Would you know this *divine energy* in your life? Observe Stephen, "full of faith and power (who), did great wonders and miracles among the people" (Acts 6:8), as he bears witness before the Jewish council that Jesus is the Christ. He crowned his testimony by laying down his life for the One who had died for him. The power of the Cross, manifest as much in the glowing face of Stephen as in the words of his message, reached out and laid hold of Saul of Tarsus. This persecutor of the Church became the apostle who above all others demonstrated the glorious message of the Cross.

In an apparent tragedy, the death of a young man just entering into a powerful ministry, we may see from the Father's point of view the Cross in three dimensions. The Cross as an operative *principle* in Stephen's life led him to declare truth in the face of well-known consequences; as a *place* it brought him into conflict with the Jewish council; and as an exploding *power* it "caught" a proud Pharisee, who found it hard "to kick against the pricks." Saul was first "caught" not only by a principle, but by living-power.

From the above object lesson, God interprets the Cross as a living principle, as a place of exposure, and finally as the power (dunamis) by which He breaks the hardest hearts and rectifies them wholly unto Himself. Such rectification is so complete that the same Cross-principle becomes operative in another life and continues like a chain-reaction. This is God's way of spontaneous expansion.

With all of this as background we shall be able to appreciate Paul's statement in 1 Corinthians 1:18. My own free and expanded translation gives this summary of the Cross in all its dimensions:

"This divine cross-principle, when expressed in mere words is utter foolishness to the man of this world who embraces a selfish way of life, but where these two ways of living come into conflict, an exposure is produced. This is the place where God released His divine energy in explosive power to utterly rectify man."

16

ONE WHO HAS for many years truly enjoyed looking out from the Father's viewpoint, has given this wise observation: "The imperative need of this hour is not so much to challenge new recruits to start on the highway of service for God — though surely that is always needed — but rather to help the multiplied hundreds scattered around the world who have started out, but have for various reasons become bewildered, defeated and side-tracked. It is not more effort, but more effectiveness that we need." Why do so very few actually allow God to realize His ultimate intention in their lives? In the coming chapters we shall hope to uncover some of the reasons why His children are ever "coming short." We are sure there are many who need to . . .

Learn These Distinctions

AS WE BEGIN TO PROGRESS along God's highway of realization with our faces turned toward Him — His pleasure, satisfaction, honor and glory, we leave multitudes of believers behind. For while many would like to think they are moving on this way they cannot move one step forward without embracing the way of the Cross. This is the life for which we have been marked out from the very beginning. There is no other highway.

Others of God's children are struggling along earnestly desiring to embrace the Cross, but are confused by things they meet in life. Many have become burdened and oppressed with false issues imposed by the enemy, who is determined to make this HIGHway impossible to traverse and other than God intended. This he cannot do if we understand what is happening to us, for God has made the way so clear that no one need stumble or go astray.

SOURCES OF DIFFICULTY

First we must learn to recognize the source of difficulty. Does it come from God, the enemy, as a result of natural factors, or from our own deliberate choice? Every step of progress necessitates making finer distinctions between things that differ. The further we go, the sharper these distinctions must become. God seems to permit this very thing in order to keep us close to Him that we may know His mind and intention in every difficulty.

Perhaps the most common types of difficulty experienced by the believer fall into four groupings: chastisement, reaping, oppression and hindrances. A believer should learn these distinctions. Chastisement is an act of God; reaping comes in the natural course of events; oppression and hindrance is from the evil one; whereas Cross-bearing is a way of life deliberately chosen by the believer who is living unto God.

"When God in love lays the rod to the back of His children, He does not ask permission," says A. W. Tozer. For the believer, chastisement is only voluntary in the sense that he chooses the will of God with the knowledge that disobedience will bring chastisement. God as our heavenly Father, has both the right and the wisdom to apply the rod as concerns our eternal welfare. While chastisement may for the moment appear grievous, there is always the *afterward* when the Father receives a mature son, and we receive the privileges of sonship. "For whom the Lord loveth He chasteneth and scourgeth every son whom He receiveth. If ye endure chastening, God dealeth with you as with sons; for what son is he whom the father chasteneth not?" (Heb. 12:6-7).

Reaping comes as the result of the natural laws of cause and effect. If you have been in the sun too long, it is natural for you to have sunburn or a headache. We might be amazed to realize how much ill in a Christian's life is retribution for foolish judgments in the light of natural laws. Nature brings its own chastisement.

Another form of difficulty experienced by believers who set their faces toward God's will and purpose is oppression or intervention of Satan. He is the hinderer and his methods are legion. Sometimes he uses affliction to beset the mind and spirit. More often he intrudes upon the sphere of our activity. Christ was always quick to recognize the source of hindrance, whether it was Peter or the enemy behind Peter. Daniel knew when his work was being hindered and delayed by the enemy. Paul was ever alert to see the hindrance of Satan. See 1 Thessalonians 2:18. Before we make much progress on *this highway of realizing God's intention*, we shall discover the importance of being occupied with our Lord, yet ever watchful and discerning of the enemy's wiles.

THE CROSS IS CHOSEN

Bearing the Cross is something different from all of these. The Cross never comes unsolicited; whereas the rod is always imposed. Some trials come as natural consequences. The enemy is always on hand to hinder without invitation. God is ever seeking those who voluntarily embrace the divine way of living regardless of the cost to self. I am convinced that it is not only *possible* to know what our Cross is, but that each believer *should* know how to recognize his particular Cross.

On the way to His Cross our Saviour cried, "Take up your Cross and follow me." He did not explain what He meant until He Himself had passed through death into the life beyond the tomb. Having ascended to the right hand of the Father, He reveals through the Apostle Paul, the meaning of His Cross, and its claims upon all who desire to follow Him.

Paul never says, "Take your Cross." He proclaims the Cross of Christ as having already triumphed. He bids the believer enter into the triumph of the Lord. Paul makes the meaning of Cross-bearing clear in 2 Corinthians 4. After describing his own ministry, he explains the

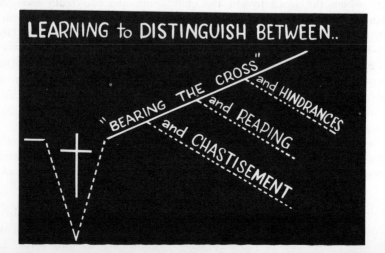

LEARNING to DISTINGUISH BETWEEN..
"BEARING THE CROSS" and HINDRANCES
and REAPING
and CHASTISEMENT

reason for the difficulties under which he preaches, "Always bearing about in the body the dying of the Lord Jesus, *that the life also of Jesus might be made manifest in our body"* Verse 10. What this means to each individual perhaps only the Holy Spirit can make real. Yet it is actually Christ once again pouring out His life in and through us *for others.*

The call to embrace the divine manner of living, which is the working of death, is a privilege which we deliberately choose. It is never imposed upon us. It is not, as is often assumed, trials, afflictions, incurable disease, the loss of money, or even the death of a loved one. To say of one of these, "This is my cross, and I must bear it for His sake," is to evidence a basic misunderstanding of the inwrought Cross.

THE CROSS CAN BE KNOWN

When a close friend asked pointedly, "What is your cross?" I had only a general idea of the subject as outlined in the discussion thus far. But when he pinpointed the question for me, I received an indelible impression by the Spirit which has marked my life.

He said, "Your cross is to fulfill that specific calling for which God has apprehended you. It comes as you live to realize that distinctive ministry for which He has prepared you. The cross is different for everyone."

I realized immediately what he meant. For years he had faced the most bitter opposition, persecution and misunderstanding while obediently following what he believed to be God's ultimate intention for his life. It was made clear to me as I observed that brother's life that a child of God who embraces the heavenly way of living can expect the abuse and misuse of people who attempt to set him at naught. When a believer sets himself to please God at any cost, the most distressing abuse is not that loosed by the powers of hell. Close friends, relatives and loved ones will feel duty bound to God to help re-direct your ways and to cause you to take a more *sane* approach to life.

No wonder Jesus warned that following Him would mean an utter detachment from all: possessions, loved ones, positions. With the Lord Jesus, who set His face toward Jerusalem that He might realize the Father's purpose, we may share the inner joy known to those who endure hardship while pressing toward the mark. When He calls, there is no other course to follow. Only by the *way of the Cross* is it possible to fulfill divine destiny. Hardship and suffering are endured joyfully by those who are being poured out for Him.

Acceptance of the way of the Cross calls for a word of caution. Be sure of the *source* of all difficulty. One of God's choice servants makes this exhortation:

"Blessed are ye" said our Lord, "when men shall revile you, and persecute you, and shall say all manner of evil against you...." But that is not all. Four other words are added: They are, *"falsely, for my sake."* These words show that the suffering must come voluntarily, that it must be chosen in the larger choice of Christ and righteousness. If the accusation men cry against me is true, no blessedness follows.

He continues. We delude ourselves when we try to turn our just punishments into a cross and rejoice over that for which we should rather repent. "For what glory is it, if, when ye be buffeted for your faults, ye shall take it patiently? but if, when ye do well, and suffer for it, ye take it patiently, that is accepted with God" (1 Peter 2:20). The Cross is always in the way of righteousness. We feel the pain of the Cross only when we suffer for Christ's sake by our own willing choice.

DISCERNING THE SOURCE

Most difficulties are to teach us some lesson; others are to be resisted as hindrances of the enemy; still others are to bring us to humility and repentance. It is very important to know then which are to be suffered with patience and even rejoicing. The believer is brought again and again to the place of prayer to inquire of the Lord concerning adversity. By wisdom received from above he discerns the *source* of his trials and responds with understanding and maturity.

As we grow in the Lord and move along in ministry for Him, we may have Paul's own testimony. "Seeing we have this ministry, we faint not" (2 Cor. 4:1). Again in verse sixteen he repeats, "We faint not ... for though our outward man perish, yet the inward man is renewed day by day ... for we look at the things which are eternal."

The *eternal viewpoint* causes present hardships to be effective in our lives as a *means to an end*. When we submit our lives wholly to the Lord, we may have assurance that nothing reaches us without His permission. In everything we are able to give thanks. The need for careful discernment is in itself a source of great blessing, for it keeps us in the place of the humble learner. The knowledge of our dependence upon the Lord brings us to follow like sheep, ever trusting the Shepherd.

All the time, in a variety of ways, our Shepherd is bringing us through experiences which are for our testing. There is reference in the first letter to the Thessalonians, where the Apostle speaks of God as, He "which trieth (or who proveth) our heart," and that, just in a very simple phrase, explains what God is doing. He is proving, putting us to the test, and seeing right down into the very center and spring of our being, how we react under that test.

From our point of view such treatment could only seem harsh. Yet the Lord always purposes that we might be approved. I believe it would help us in many of our circumstances and experiences, if we could have this key by which to interpret. It is not only possible, but it is His intention that we should emerge strengthened and approved. But it is sadly possible for the people of God under trial to be disapproved.

Perhaps the most difficult thing for most folk is to recognize that some testings are purely on a spiritual basis quite apart from any circumstances. For example, there may descend upon us, a kind of darkness, a kind of apathy; more than that, a despair, a heaviness, a sense of the unreality of things. This becomes for us a spiritual testing-ground, as to whether we accept or whether we will rise against it and refuse to live in such an atmosphere. What a liberation was mine when I realized that God did not intend for me to be smothered in such a "heavy atmosphere." In overcoming it is important to realize that it is not the circumstances but the atmosphere which must be changed.

THIS FINAL CAUTION

Let us beware of self-made crosses. We need never go out of our way to find them, and those which we make for ourselves are double crosses, because being outside the will of God, they bring no strength, consolation or fruit. Such are all crosses which arise from uneasy fears about the future. We have no right to anticipate His dispensations, or attempt to supply the place of His providence by a providence of our own. (John Gregory Mantle in THE WAY OF THE CROSS.)

17

FROM THE BEGINNING we have been concerned with three things: (1) having a proper starting point; (2) having all the parts fit into a proper framework of reference; (3) having our attention properly focused on His ultimate intention.

Now as we continue looking out from His viewpoint we see how men through the centuries have always run effectively when their eyes were set on His goal. While there may seem to be many goals, for the one who is truly centered in God, there really is only HIS GOAL. Let us consider three laws which are always operative in His sons who are . . .

Running the Race
to Reach the Goal

WE MUST BE CAREFUL not to exhort men to run the race before they have been placed on *the race track*. It is important to make the distinction (as on the blackboard) that we must first experience God's grace in receiving the *gift of Life;* then and only then can we begin to run the race in fulfilling the purpose of our life and reaching His goal.

Generally there are two groups which misunderstand this: Those unregenerate people who attempt to run before they have experienced His grace and assume that getting to heaven or achieving salvation is the goal; and those who know they have received the gift of eternal life by grace, yet have not been enlightened to see how they are called to run the race to reach the goal of their "high calling." Both groups emphasize parts which are not properly related to the whole plan. Since we have considered grace (part A) let us now focus our attention on the need of a goal in running the race.

THE POWER OF A GOAL

Consider an individual who has his eye set on scaling the world's highest mountain. This is his life's ambition—his only goal. After repeated failures he finally succeeds and triumphantly stands in the rarefied air of his accomplishment, his mission achieved. Now no other goal lies before him. What is the effect?

First reflect on the planning, the physical training, the growth in strength that accrued to him so long as his goal was before him. Now consider the fading interest, the physical weakness, the unrestrained living, and atrophy which follow because there is no pull or power of a goal to challenge him.

Again, consider a people who are captivated with the need of a church building. They are strangely united as they overcome obstacles and dedicate time and resources to achieve their goal. Finally their object is realized. On dedication Sunday they move into the church and settle down to enjoy their labors. With no other goal before them, they soon become soft in their moral fiber, and careless in their dedication. Since dedication was to a goal, but not to HIS GOAL, nothing fails like success.

It would be well at this point to recognize not only the symptoms, but the cause of breakdown in purpose in the lives of individuals and congregations. Many have allowed certain goals to become the end

A- In Accepting His Grace –
We receive the gift

B- In Running the Race
We reach the goal

THE GIFT ← - - - - "B" - - - - → THE GOAL
① ② ③

"A"

Three Essential Laws for
Running the Race
① - POWER
② - PERCEPTION
③ - PERSPECTIVE

instead of means to an ultimate goal – HIS PURPOSE. They have obtained the assurance of salvation and settled down; they have arrived at a separated life and settled down; they have experienced the filling and anointing of the Spirit and settled down. Having achieved their new building, their attendance quota, their missionary budget – there is nothing more to live for. They have been dedicated to a project or some person instead of THE PERSON. There is far more concern for *receiving* the grace of God, than living to *give* and thereby to find the fuller meaning of life.

When there is no supreme goal or spiritual purpose, people generally concentrate on motion. Instead of working toward ultimate fulfillment of the Father's intention, they keep changing their goals and call this progress. They do not know where they are going, but they are certainly *on their way*. Those who find no clear meaning or destiny in life really can never say they are making progress in the race. If there is no fixed course and destination, they can never measure whether they are getting to their goal or not. Life under such circumstances is boring and meaningless. Let us not be like the sculptor who was hacking and cutting away at a block of marble all day. When he was asked, "What are you making?" he said, "I really don't know, I haven't seen the plans."

PERCEPTION OF THE GOAL

This leads us to ask the important question, "How much does God intend to reveal to us of His plans?" Are we to work blindly but devotedly confident that He, the Master Architect, knows what He is doing and all we need is to get orders sufficient for each day? That might be ample for servants, but we are *sons* who are called to share and reign in that *great day* when the sons of God are revealed. Surely God intends to unveil not only the principles but also the patterns by which He works when we are ready and our perception is increased.

We find here a law of God's working. First He gives us the "bud," and as our power of perception increases it blossoms into the full flowering of our place in His ultimate intention. Let us observe this in four examples. In each, whether Abraham, Israel, Paul, or the Church, we see God sharing His intention in a nutshell, then ever waiting to unfold His intention as men walk in obedience. How much did they understand in the beginning? We can be sure it was sufficient to pull them toward His goal. In each case there is continuous revelation to bring progress toward reaching the goal.

THE GOAL UNFOLDS

(1) When our Father God called Abraham to be the earthly shadow of Himself, it was first indicated to him that he would be the *father* of many nations. Yet it was many years before Abraham was able to comprehend all God meant in those initial words. Finally, after many and devious experiences, in the hour of his supreme dedication of Isaac on Mount Moriah, we see Abraham's eyes opened to perceive God's goal. In the measure that he walked in obedience, this purpose was realized through him.

(2) Consider how God sought to make Israel responsive to His goal. Having delivered her from Egypt, He speaks at Mount Sinai indicating Israel was to be a "kingdom of priests, a holy nation and a peculiar treasure unto (Him)" (Ex. 19:5-6). Yet through repeated disobediences, we see her perceptive powers numbed. She faltered in the race. Paul uses Israel (in 1 Cor. 9) as both an example and a warning, so we will not miss God's ultimate intention as she did.

"Know ye not that they which run in a race run all, but one receiveth the prize? So run that ye may obtain. And every man that striveth for mastery is temperate in all things. Now they do it to obtain a corruptible crown; but we an incorruptible" (1 Cor. 9:24-25).

Of course Paul is not here considering salvation. He is showing how Israel, though delivered from Egypt, wandered in the wilderness and failed to realize the purpose God had set for her. Paul is not speaking of losing the gift of salvation. He is concerned lest (like Israel) he become a castaway and fail to fulfill God's ultimate intention.

(3) Consider Paul. Immediately after his Damascus road experience, Ananias spoke in prophesy over him indicating the calling and ministry for which God had set him apart. This was what God gave in bud form to unfold in the great Apostle's life. Finally in Philippians 3, we hear him share his deep purpose to reach the goal of this race course. "Brothers, I do not consider myself to have won it; but ONE THING I DO—forgetting the past, and straining to those in front, I rush along the track for the prize of the supreme calling of God in Christ Jesus" (Phil. 3:13-14, F. Fenton).

It was the clear declaration of the goal which pulled him; nor are we left in any doubt as to his perception. He knew where he was going. But Paul is never concerned just for himself. How typical is his further admonition: "And if in anything ye be otherwise minded, God shall reveal even this unto you" (verse 15). Paul hands them a measuring stick for evaluating their own attitude in the race. If they are living for a lesser goal than he, as their pattern is living, they can expect God to make it known to them.

(4) Finally, consider the exhortation to the Church. Through Paul, God shared His glorious intention that His Son should have a *body* through which to express Himself. This is the glorious calling and destiny of the Church. The question is, does she perceive the goal of her Lord? She has been given the bud of promise, but we wonder why the flower is so slow to blossom. It would seem that the writer.of the Hebrews was concerned about this question. He reminds us of all the past runners in the race who are now looking down upon the race course: "Wherefore seeing we also are compassed about with so great a cloud of witnesses, let us lay aside every weight, and the sin which doth so easily beset us, and let us run with patience the RACE THAT IS SET BEFORE US" (Hebrews 12:1).

Throughout the Epistle to the Hebrews we have this ringing exhortation constantly before us: *let us go on* to reach full maturity which only comes in living unto God and realizing His ultimate intention.

GOAL IN PERSPECTIVE

Still another law governs our running of the race—the law of spiritual perspective. To the natural eye something in the distance seems small and unimportant, while everything close by looms very large and impressive.

Suppose you look down a long row of telephone poles. The pole by which you are standing seems very large; the one on the distant horizon appears to be only a pinpoint in comparison. It seems to be true; your eyes tell you it is true, and yet it is not true. If you will get into your automobile and drive to that exact point on the horizon and have another look, you will find that some almost unbelievable changes have taken place. The telephone pole which once had such great importance in your eyes has now become small and insignificant, whereas the one you once thought appeared of no consequence has now doubled in size and importance many times. What a few miles back appeared to be the least of the telephone poles has now become the most important one of all.

This illustrates the deception of looking at things in the natural. That which is seen and temporal can make distant, spiritual goals seem small. It is only when spiritual eye-salve has been applied that we can see according to His perspective. Paul wrote from God's perspective when he said, "For our light affliction (the nearest telephone pole) which is but for a moment, worketh for us a far more exceeding and eternal weight of glory; while we look not at the things which are seen: for the things which are seen are temporal; but the things which are not seen are eternal" (2 Cor. 4:18).

You may have tried this interesting experiment. A nickel placed over your eye will blot out the biggest star. A quarter will blot out the sun. Of course, that does not mean the quarter is larger than the sun. It is just closer to your eye.

This deception, which applies to space, also applies to time. If you have a six-year-old son who has a financial problem, you may test his perspective by asking him which he would rather have, a quarter today, or a dollar next month. Unless he is a very unusual boy, the quarter right now will loom much larger in his eyes than the dollar appears when placed thirty days in the future.

You will remember that this is the kind of deception that got Esau into trouble. One night Esau came home hungry. Jacob said, "Esau, if you will assign to me all the lands, cattle, goods and properties contained in your birthright, I will give you a mess of pottage." From the perspective of one who has just had a good dinner, that proposition seems a little bit ridiculous. But Esau was hungry, and hunger can change one's perspective so that a mess of pottage seems exceedingly important.

I suppose Esau thought, "What difference does it make what happens tomorrow, if I am hungry right now." It is possible for almost any small, unimportant "want" to be held so close to the eyes as to blot out the entire future purpose of God. I can hardly fathom what "a mess of pottage" really is. It has never sounded very appetizing to me, but Esau gave up his entire future to obtain one.

There is a divine perspective which God has always shared with those who walk in His light. "In thy light we shall see light" (Ps. 36:9). Walking in His light will help us not only to keep every telephone pole (experience) in perfect alignment, but also to keep each in God's divine perspective. This means every lesser goal will telescope into His ultimate goal. The man of vision is one who can see telephone poles on the horizon in the same scale as they will appear when he actually gets to them. He lives with the power, the perception and the perspective of HIS GOAL.

JOY IS THE ONE THING most evident in those who have been caught by the heavenly way and purpose of life. They have learned to live in the strength and source of JOY, Himself. As our Lord Jesus, the forerunner in the race, ran with joy, so we shall see, Paul and today's triumphant Christians experience joy in all three tenses: past, present and future. We are called to joy. It is not optional but imperative that everyone who runs to win should exhibit . . .

Joy: The Mark of Maturity

IN CONTINUING OUR THEME, running the race, let us turn our attention to the One who has already finished His course. Because Jesus is the Author (both the starter and the finisher), He is our confidence that we too can finish the race "in Him."

"Looking unto Jesus, the author and finisher of our faith; who FOR THE JOY that was set before Him ENDURED THE CROSS, despising the shame, and is set down at the right hand of the throne of God" (Heb. 12:2).

There are several phrases here which attract our attention. Let those who have considered *the way of the Cross* as something impossible, look at Jesus. Look first at the JOY THAT WAS SET BEFORE HIM and you will understand how He ENDURED THE CROSS. It was because He had His eyes, not on the pathway, but on the goal. When the goal is important enough to us, any pathway becomes a secondary consideration. It was because He lived with His eye on the future—the glorious anticipation of the joy He might bring to His Father, and the fulness of joy which He might then share with His brethren—that Jesus endured the Cross.

I shall never forget the days in my life when, with all my heart I sought to live the *way of the Cross*. My death with Christ had become so real to me. I longed to embrace the working of death in order that life might flow out to others. But my zeal without proper understanding repulsed people instead of drawing them. One night after a service I overheard some of my youthful friends whom I wanted so much to help. They were talking about me. "What has happened to him? Once he was full of fun. Now all he keeps talking about is the Cross and death. He's become a deadpan with no personality."

I was stunned. Was this the impression I was giving? I went to my room and convinced myself that such was the lot of any who would dare to embrace the inwrought Cross. And it was not until several months later that the Holy Spirit was able to show me another important distinction. I learned there is a great difference between the *sentence of death* and the *spirit of death*. I knew, indeed, that I was to reckon on identification with Christ in His death and that now God had placed the sentence of death on all my members. But I came to see this did not mean I was to bear the spirit of death.

This simple distinction wrought an emancipation in my spirit. I saw that once we have been raised with Christ from the tomb, the sentence of death remains upon the old, but must not touch the new life and spirit. We are to be under the control of the Spirit of life and joy. How different it was to be free from the shadow of the old and to allow Christ to reflect Himself through my personality.

THE PAST . . . JOY IN REMEMBRANCE

The believer in Christ has a past, but he is joyful because it is truly past. One thing so evident in those who have been liberated from their gnawing conscience and slavery to sin is that they dare to talk about the past. No one enjoys talking about bondage that is still present with him. There is no joy in "holding out to the bitter end" in order to be saved. Once we know the grace of God, we know the joy of sins forgiven. There are many passages which show that redemption gives us the privilege of being joyful. "Let us enJOY the peace we have with God" (Rom. 5:1, Moffatt). Some have peace with God but have never entered into the enjoyment of it—for they are still straining and sweating while depending upon themselves. Another passage reads,

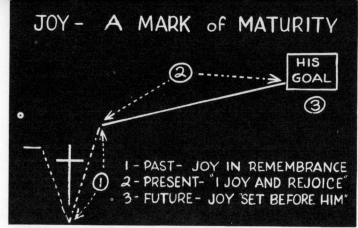

"We enjoy our redemption" (Eph. 1:7, Moffatt). To be redeemed and not enjoy that redemption seems like a contradiction of terms. Again, "We both enjoy our access to the Father in one Spirit" (Eph. 2:18), Moffatt). One who understood this said, "My greatest joy is in something beyond joy but which includes joy—free access to the Father."

THE PRESENT . . . PARTICIPATION IN JOY

We must be sure that we have distinguished true joy from its counterfeits. There is a happiness which initiates from happenings. This is not true joy. There is an exuberance which springs from the dynamic of the soulish powers, but this is not true joy. True joy has its source in God and flows through those who have learned the abiding union.

In every life there is a point at which the believer comes out of sighings and begins rejoicing. And if he doesn't, he has stopped short on the race track. I think you will discover the sighing state continues in those who have never been laid hold of by the perception of God's ultimate intention. When a believer doesn't see the future joy which is set before him, he finds no joy in the present in which to participate. This is not so much the sighing over sin or the need for personal victory, as it is a sighing in the work; a deep inward sighing because the heart longs for a greater fruitfulness.

This is a snare we must avoid. It should not be our work, but His. If it is our work, and we are getting satisfaction from the work itself, we have not learned that He is to become both the source and joy of our work.

Paul could have sung the blues because only Timothy was really like-minded and living unto the furtherance of the gospel. Yet, even amid falling away, he was constantly rejoicing. He says: "I have learned to be independent of circumstances which might render what I know in my mind ineffective in my life; I have learned that my resources (in Him) are sufficient and that my poise is undisturbable"

(Phil. 4:11-12, Moffatt). It is no wonder that even from a prison cell Paul can make joy the central theme of his letter.

We can understand why Rendell Harris says: "Joy is the strength of the people of God; it is their chief characteristic." If you allow the spirit of depression to settle, it saps strength even when nothing is done. How I have loved the lines penned by one in China. No one can doubt this missionary wife had been lifted up into God and her viewpoint synchronized with His. She moved and breathed in the Eternal.

> "Lord, I belong here at your side,
> Singing Your song, swinging Your stride,
> JOY SURGING with the strength of a tide."

> Since I've been running the race with Thee,
> Every note is tuned to your major key,
> LIFE HAS BECOME A GRAND SYMPHONY.

Many do not expect union with Christ to make them basically and fully joyful now. Such joy they believe to be reserved for the hereafter. But Paul writes to Timothy, of God, "Who richly provides us with all the joys of life" (1 Tim. 6:17, Moffatt). Notice that he says, "all the joys of life" *now*. You do not have to go outside Christ to presently participate in all the joys. It is these which He "richly provides."

THE FUTURE . . . JOY IN ANTICIPATION

For those who are not enjoying the present participation in His joy, we suggest that failure to anticipate the joy of the future is probably the reason. A little ten-year-old girl caught the true meaning of joy. "Daddy," she said, "I seem to have the most joy when I bring joy to you." Her joy had become a creative thing; something enjoyable now, but also in anticipation. Joy is not sought; it seeks us when we are creative, outgoing and living unto the ultimate.

This joy of anticipation is of a particular kind. It is best represented in the Lord Jesus: who "for the joy that was set before him endured. . . ." It was not the joy of what happened *to Him*, but of what happened *through Him*. It was joy which was creative in its nature. If we think of joy resulting from what happens to us—people giving us gifts, or holding us in high esteem—then ours is not true joy, but something immature and precarious. Anything, including joy, is off-centered when it is ego-centric. Such joy cannot abide. Since this is true, maturity depends upon our being objective instead of subjective—outgoing instead of self-relating.

When John says, "And we are writing this that your joy may be complete," he is speaking of the joy of realizing that God through him will unfold some of His purposes. It was not merely something he wanted to happen for him, but through him. This is the difference between passing happiness and abiding joy.

When Paul writes "... even if my life is being poured as a libation upon the sacrificial offering of your faith, ... I joy and rejoice ... " it was because of what God was doing through him. He adds, "And I bid you also to joy and rejoice."

How different is this from the testimony of those who plead for prayers that they may be faithful in running the race. The sad, morose type of person who complains about the troubles of being a Christian reveals that something is wrong within. He is filled with inner conflicts and wrong attitudes toward life. Joy comes as the result of inner harmony.

When there is no civil war within; when everything is under a single control and directed toward a single purpose, then joy is a natural concomitant. You do not seek it, it is there inherently, and it is there permanently, for it does not come and go. The conditions that produce it are an integral part of life. We don't have joy, it has us.

19

AS WE ARE CONTINUING in His viewpoint, we come now to another reason many stop short in continuing to run the race on God's HIGHWAY. We are amazed how many still carry the spirit of fear or duty into their service; others are motivated by the hope of personal gain. These motives are not acceptable for living "unto God" and for realizing His ultimate intention. Our heavenly Father is not concerned merely for the labor done, but for His sons. Far more than service, He desires sons who share His Spirit, love and purpose in . . .

Living Under a New Government

THERE ARE THREE LEVELS of human living — three possible motives by which we might try to serve the Lord. Let us illustrate this by using a simple story from a slave market.

A young colored lad was on the block. His parents had just been sold. Suddenly a hush fell over the crowd as every eye was turned toward a stranger who kept bidding persistently although the price already exceeded that which was normal. What could the stranger see in the ragged youngster on the block?

One could almost read the questions on the faces of those who stood by. What did he want with this whisp of humanity? Who was he? Why should he pay so much? Finally the auctioneer cried, "Sold!" Eagerly they watched the purposeful stranger elbow his way to the center to receive his property. A scene followed that the observers would never forget.

Immediately the slave buyer pressed a hastily written paper into the laddie's hand. "This is yours," he said "It means you are free." Free? What did freedom mean to the child of a slave? In answer to the large, questioning eyes, the buyer explained. "I saw your mammy and pappy—how your family was about to be broken, so I bought you to set you free. You won't need to come with me; you may go along with your family."

Somehow the impact of it gripped him—he understood. He was free! He stood looking from the kindly stranger to his mother and father. The struggle of the boy's heart showed in his questioning eyes. The strange massah had paid the highest price to let him go free? Such a man must be very good. One could safely trust in him. Suddenly the strippling lad was off the block, and casting himself before his friend he said, "Massah, yo' bought me fo' sech a price, I knows I'll nevah find anotha like you." He handed back the piece of paper. "Don't make me go back to be sole again. Ole Massah'd nevah mind 'dat papah. I'd rathah be your slave 'till I dies." The lad, overcome by the the stranger's kindness clung to his knees until a big hand reached down to lift him up.

This incident illustrates, as we have pictured on the blackboard, three levels of life in which we may live. First, the boy stood in slavery. He was under the control of his master, who represented "outward law." His serving was by the spirit of fear or duty. Then he became free of the "outward law"—the slave master. In our story this freedom was short, for the pull of a higher law gripped him and he immediately chose to be a captive of love. Thus he moved to the highest level of service by exchanging his own freedom for the higher law of love. *Freedom has become his to give away.* It was like moving from one captivity to another.

Here is a principle which seems to govern all God's dealings with man. When Adam first appeared in the lovely Garden of Eden, he was placed on that middle level: in freedom. The choice before him was either to become a love slave "unto God," or to become a captive "under law." Ever since Adam turned to his own selfish way, the entire human race has needed outward law to curb its selfish inclinations. It would be wonderful if we could begin, as Adam did, in that middle level of freedom. But every one, because of his inward bent toward selfishness and rebellion against God, needs a Saviour to lift him from his slavery and sin. This was the purpose in the finished work of Christ on Calvary which provided for the liberation of every

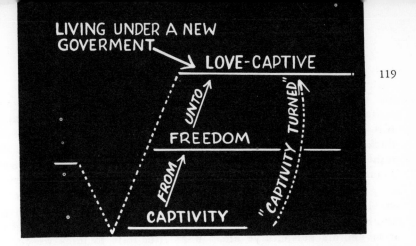

LIVING UNDER A NEW GOVERMENT

LOVE-CAPTIVE

UNTO

FREEDOM

"CAPTIVITY TURNED"

FROM

CAPTIVITY

man who will receive of God's grace—the price has been paid by Another.

But it is just at this point that religious men and methods have turned God's grace into disgrace. It is the same old humanistic story. Being more concerned for man than God, they have so emphasized man's *freedom from* that they have allowed selfish men to accept the doctrine without the explosive revelation ever touching their lives. Our churches are filled with "converts" who have a delightful mental understanding of the doctrine of freedom, but who have never known the Holy Spirit's unveiling of their self-centeredness and continued slavery *to their own ways*. A true understanding of God's grace will always "turn our captivity."

LIVING IN THE TRANSITION

Too many, it would seem, have imagined that freedom is a goal, as though coming into this transition zone (freedom) was all that God intended. Paul clarifies the issue when he insists, because of the mercy of God in setting us free *from*, we ought now to present our bodies as a living sacrifice *unto Him*. As it was with the colored lad, so it should be with us. We should remain in the passing zone of personal freedom just long enough to choose to come under the higher law of love. We have every reason to believe that had the lad taken his freedom "for himself" it would have been just a short time before some slavemaster would have taken him into bondage. He must have something to *use his freedom for*. We will either invest our freedom by yielding unto the Lord Jesus, or we will invite further slavery as we attempt to keep our freedom for ourselves.

I wonder if this is not the real point of Paul's exhortation to the Galatians. On the verge of turning back to the system and spirit of the law as the rule of action for their lives, they heard stern words of counsel from their father in the gospel. "In this (new) freedom Christ has made us... completely free; stand fast then... and do not submit again to a yoke of slavery which you have once put off" (Gal. 5:1 A.N.T.). In other words, Paul is warning, "Don't be so foolish as to think that you have anything to gain by turning back to the law. Move into the new and glorious plane where the law of the Spirit reigns." Actually, he reminds them, there is no middle position where we can long remain. "If ye be led of the Spirit ye are not under the law." As surely as we attempt to use freedom for ourselves, we are inviting another more subtle slavery — slavery to self. "To whom ye yield your members, his servants ye are." What utter folly to think we can very long live — in the *transition zone!*

LIVING UNDER A NEW GOVERNMENT

What is more tragic than this present-day man-centered ministry which seems only concerned for what man can get from God. Many speak loudly of God's grace but fail to recognize its full divine implications. We have been pointing out, how from the very beginning Adam and his family have made the choice either to live under outward law or to have the law written in their hearts, which means they come under the government of His Spirit. It is in this sense that we can enter now into the government of His kingdom, even before the Lord Jesus comes to set up His visible reign. We do not need to wait until the kingdom age to come under the law of the kingdom. Throughout every dispensation since Adam, there have been those who entered the race to live unto His ultimate intention. It is the delight of our Father that He will one day have many sons who are one with Him in Spirit, love, dedication, vision and realization.

Dr. A. T. Schofield of London tells how his dog, Jack, learned about this government. Used to running on a leash, when taken on the street by his master, the dog was one day given freedom. At first he bounded away in complete unrestraint. Suddenly he discovered that being away from his master was a fearful experience. He was used to walking close enough to hear his master's voice. The man's spirit seemed to have penetrated his dog consciousness to form a bond he could not escape. The world outside the sphere of his owner's control was big, noisy and terrifying. The leash was gone, but now there was a new kind of government. In the new bond the dog found all the liberty he desired.

Jack the dog, illustrates so well what happens as our heavenly Father is child-training those who will one day be ready for the full-adoption of mature sons. Early in our ministry it seemed we were far more conscious of the Holy Spirit as a chain leading us. In those days we were occupied with His commands. Although attempting to run on His Highway, we were still dominated by a legal spirit.

Then the day came when He opened our eyes to see there was actually no chain in this new spirit of service. We were free. And like Jack, we bounded off to accomplish a dozen projects — we thought — for Him. At first it seemed we would enjoy the liberty of this serving. It gave us such room for our own self-expression and the feeding of our own interests. But alas, we discovered we were alone — alone in the projects we had started.

NOT OUR DOING . . . BUT HIS

How often at the close of a meeting someone will confide: "Thank you for that word; I'm determined to try harder to live under His government." I always answer: "Don't, for when you are determined to move, you move on the basis of yourself — *you* are still the center. Your serving is self-centered effort; therefore from the wrong center. God must be the center — not you. As long as God is on the margin of our trying, He is only reference, not resource."

Finally, like Jack, we must come back to His side — convinced that our "freedom jaunts" have never realized anything for Him — only for ourselves. Then by deliberate choice we choose to be led by the invisible bond — His Spirit guiding our spirit. We delight to do "THY WILL." Controlled by a Master, the Holy Spirit, we are held by a bond that has penetrated our very being. Thus we become alive to all that sonship really means: the imbibing of the very Spirit of the Father. "As many as are led by the Spirit, they are the (mature) sons of God."

How the Father longs to emancipate His children that they might walk, not in the letter, but in the Spirit, where they can enjoy the glorious liberty of the sons of God.

Finally, we must be sure we have understood what God intends in this liberty. Liberty and freedom are words on every tongue and yet no concept is more misunderstood. Most everyone thinks of being free *from* something, but rarely of being free *for* something. Men seem to feel they are free only because they have no ball and chain on their feet, but they have little concern for why God has planned freedom. How differently freedom appears from His viewpoint as we shall see in the coming lesson.

20

APART FROM HIS VIEWPOINT the real purpose of God will always be missed. We must view all history, whether of Israel or of the Church, from the divine viewpoint in order to grasp the unique part each plays in the Father's plan. If we become engrossed in lesser details it is possible to miss the thread of divine purpose which runs through the earthly pilgrimage of God's chosen people. When we consider the reasons for their continued falling and rising, we are sure they never have wholly grasped what it would mean to have their . . .

Captivity Turned

ISRAEL NEEDED CONTINUOUS revelation from God. Her waxing and waning as a nation was determined by her sense of vision, purpose, and divine destiny. When each rising generation forgot the faith and vision of their fathers, decline was inevitable. Proverbs 29:18 tells us why. In various translations the verse reads:

"Where there is no vision, the people perish"—King James version.
"Where there is no vision . . . people cast off restraint. . ."—Darby
"Without revelation a nation fades."—F. Fenton

When we take God's panoramic view of Israel, we see the sad history of a people always ready for help in times of oppression and adversity but never quite ready to be used of Him. Again and again Israel cried out for deliverance and was set free. Yet each time she failed to interpret what God was really doing. She seemed far more interested in what God could *do for her* in her time of need, than in what she could *do* or *be for Him* when she was free.

On the blackboard we have pictured five periods of Israel's history. Five times she was delivered in order to move toward her divine destiny; but five times she seemed blind to God's ultimate purpose and fell into another time of captivity.

First, we find Israel in Egyptian bondage. Not until the taskmasters' severe oppression became unbearable did she think of God, the source of her deliverance. In due time she was set free. Across the Red Sea, at Mount Sinai, God proposed the next step. Will Israel now be UNTO HIM a holy nation, a royal priesthood and a peculiar people? Quite glibly she answers, "Yes." Yet the whole course of history reveals that, as was Adam from the beginning, she was far more interested in *getting* than in *being* or *giving* all God intended.

Again we find her taken captive by fear in the wilderness. She wandered forty years while the fearful generation died off. When she finally liberated across the Jordan in order to possess Canaan land *for God*, she soon settled down to possess it *for herself*. Using her freedom and God's provision for her own enjoyment, she became captive to the nations of Canaan.

Once again Israel cried to God for help and this time He raised up judges and deliverers. Again she forgot who had delivered her from Egypt, provided for her in the wilderness and led her into Canaan. When God granted her desire for a king, she soon turned the kingdom of David and Solomon to her own glory. Then in His wrath, God allowed Israel's dispersion by Assyria followed by Judah's captivity by Babylon.

Finally the seventy years of Babylonian captivity were passed and

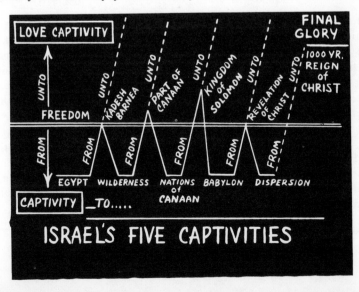

ISRAEL'S FIVE CAPTIVITIES

God liberated Judah to return to Canaan. With what joy a small portion of them came back. Now, will His people live unto Him? We know the story of their disobedience and subsequent rejection of the promised Messiah for whom Israel had waited so long. Since she would not be captive *unto Him*, she must fall into captivity to others.   At last destroyers came, Jerusalem was razed and God's people were carried away to be scattered throughout the world. What a contrast is to be seen between Israel's repeated disobedience and failure, and God's mercy and continued deliverance. What was wrong? She was interested in *using His grace*, but was indifferent to her calling and destiny.

Today God's people are in world-wide dispersion. What suffering and shame they have experienced through the centuries. But behold, a new and unique thing is about to take place. According to divine promise, God will soon intervene again—this time with finality. He will not only bring Israel back from world-wide dispersion, but He will effect an ultimate turning of her captivity. In Deuteronomy 30:3 we read of this final restoration, "...then the Lord thy God will TURN THY CAP-tivity, and have compassion upon thee, and will return and gather thee from the nations whither the Lord...hath scattered thee."

What is our lesson in all of this? For years I studied the various captivities of Israel, yet somehow never realized just how God sought for a people who would walk with Him in *continuous revelation*. The whole pilgrimage of Israel — her failures and deliverances —teach us five principles of God's dealings with His people.

THESE PRINCIPLES

(1) His grace is demonstrated that we might be free *from* captivity, but this freedom is to be used *for* and *unto* His ultimate intention.

(2) God always asks that which is impossible to the natural man in order that His people will be dependent upon divine, spiritual resources.

(3) God designs all things to function properly under His control. He is not content to merely set us free, but longs to "turn our captivity"; that is, He longs to bring us back into *His* captivity.

(4) Man must either submit to God's purpose or become captive to some other law. God's plan will not allow us to live long in liberty apart from law.

(5) God's pattern is not spurts of consecration and dedication, but a consistent walk leading into a continuous unfolding revelation of His plan and purpose.

History shows victorious Israel ever relying on God's miracle-working power; self-willed Israel continually seeking deliverance through her own schemes and alliances; captive Israel crying out in humility for deliverance from the oppressor. Deliverance was *always* through obedience to God's methods and was miraculous. It was never through the power of numbers, arms, alliances, reliance on human wisdom, or learning. In order to be delivered from adversity, Israel must submit to the "foolishness" of God which is beyond the comprehension of men.

Throughout the centuries God has found those who allowed themselves to be captured by His purpose. Christ's disciples submitted to a way of life so irregular in the eyes of contemporaries as to bring them into jeopardy day and night. Paul became a bond slave of Christ, though the worldly mind considered him to be a madman. Think it not strange today, when new purpose, philosophy, and vision of destiny floods the mind of a "captured" man, if he is set apart as a fool or a madman. As the world drinks deeply at the fountain of human error and God's own people stray farther and farther from His ultimate purpose, "madness" will even more frequently be offered as the explanation for the exploits of God's captives. In His captivity God's people will at last find perfect freedom and joy. King David describes this as follows:

> "When the Lord turned again the captivity of Zion,
>   we were like them that dream.
> Then was our mouth filled with laughter
>   and our tongue with singing.
> Then said they among the heathen,
>   'The Lord hath done great things for them!'
> The Lord hath done great things for us;
>   whereof we are glad.
> Turn again our captivity, O Lord,
>   as the streams of the south.
> They that sow in tears will reap in joy.
> He that goeth forth and weepeth,
>   bearing precious seed,
> Shall doubtless come again with rejoicing,
>   bringing his sheaves with him."
> —Psalm 126

Weeping is not usually considered, these days, to be the badge of the successful Christian worker. But David linked it with a turning of captivity. And so it has been with God's chosen ones through the centuries. Though outward circumstances give no evidence of joy and freedom, God's people still know the joy and freedom of ultimate living.

This is the very reason for our triumph. "Who shall separate us from the love of Christ? Shall tribulation, or distress, or persecution, or famine, or nakedness, or peril, or sword?" These things can be relied upon to bring captivity and defeat to all others, but God's people have joy and freedom that is not touched by circumstance. Such was the experience of Paul and John and all the apostles, and such has been the experience of hundreds and thousands of Christians who have followed in their train. The words of Ter Stegen written under severe persecution reveal the difference between being free from outward oppression and having captivity turned.

> "Need I that a law should bind me,
>   Captive unto Thee?
> Captive is my heart rejoicing,
>   Never to be free."

21

ONLY AS WE UNDERSTAND the Father's ultimate intention to have a glorious family for Himself, can we appreciate the great issues involved in the turning of Job's captivity. Here is one of God's choice sons. As he became a test-case, the Father demonstrated how He will vindicate Himself and His actions before the whole universe of man and angels. He will silence the accusing hosts of Satan, and at the same time He will call forth praise from His vast family like unto the voice of many waters: "Our God is truly a worthy Father." First let us turn to that meeting in the heavenlies when Satan accused God and . . .

The Challenge is Made

ONE DAY IN the heavenlies when the "sons of God" came to present themselves before the throne, Satan also came among them. It is noteworthy that it was the Lord who took the initiative to speak to Satan. "In thy coming and going throughout the earth...hast thou considered my servant Job that there is none like him in all the earth?" It seems strange that God should call Job to the attention of Satan, and set him up as a target for attack. Yet the Father already knew what Job's reaction would be in the crucible of testing.

Further, it seems God knew the complaint that rankled in Satan's heart as he appeared before God along with the heavenly beings. By calling Job to his attention, God brought into the open Satan's festering quarrel. The accuser responded immediately to the opportunity to unleash his hatred for God by questioning Job's real allegiance. Pointing to an apparent flaw in their relationship, he poses a taunting question, "Doth Job serve God for naught?" The adversary's reply to the Lord showed he had already considered Job to some sinister purpose. He not only cast sneering doubt on Job's character, but brought God's character into question. "You bribe men to follow you! Who wouldn't give allegiance in return for protection and every heart's desire?" His ugly challenge intimates, "God cannot fashion a family such as He ultimately intends without using bribery."

DOES GOD BRIBE MEN?

The central issue of the attack simply stated is this: "Can our Father really win sons to Himself without using 'pie-in-the-sky' bribes?" The accusation must be answered. Is it true that God must appeal to man's selfishness in order to achieve His purpose? Are His sons to be pampered and spoiled? This is a bold challenge and blast against the holiness of God. Satan—who makes *his* appeal to pride, to fear, to the sensual, and the desire for gain—taunts God with the accusation that He must use similar methods. Himself filled with infamous schemes for gaining a following, Satan accuses God of similar methods. Such is our adversary.

The basic issue in Job's case centers in the divine-human relationship. Does Job belong to God for Himself, or only for himself? Satan insinuated that Job was motivated by his own welfare, and not by a desire for God's glory and purpose. He continues the challenge: "You have a hedge around him and have blessed the work of his hands." Satan reasons from the measure of his own heart that Job was interested in God mostly because He had prospered and pampered him with so many good things. In fact Satan went so far as to suggest, "Just let me at him and we'll see what his real loyalties are." God responded by removing the hedge, but sparing only Job's life.

So all of creation was invited to observe the arena where Job was brought to trial. Angels, demons and the sons of men were called to look at the spectacle. And for centuries to follow, men have pitied poor Job and wondered why God allowed him to suffer so. Those who have identified themselves with Christ so as to share His heavenly vantage point understand what happened there. We can almost hear them saying, "What a privilege to be selected by God; to have the circumstances of life ordered by Him, so the way of adversity and suffering becomes the way to bring Him glory, honor and worship. HE ALONE IS WORTHY!"

We must remember, it is only from the side of Satan and man that the divine-human relationship is in question. There is never a question on God's part, for the Father knows each one of His own. He had already looked down the corridor of time to see Job fully rectified — His captivity turned. Satan did not initiate the case. God precipitated the crisis that was to establish Job and quiet the accusing voices of Satan's dark kingdom. Not only so, but God's victory in Job has also given occasion for the hosts of heaven to sing the glorious anthem of praise to One who brings sons to Himself because of *who He is*, and not just because of *what He does*.

JOB PROVES NO BRIBES ARE NEEDED

To the casual observer, poor Job was but a lamb led to the slaughter. Such is man's viewpoint. The enemy made it appear that it was not Job but God who was on trial. Does a just and righteous God deliberately allow His own children to suffer? Job's life became a battleground on which the Father demonstrated that He will win a vast family into love-captivity without appealing to the hope of personal gain or the fear of loss.

The One who has never spared Himself would not spare Job, but allowed him to go through tests which were to purify his motives. God depends upon none of the selfish motivations commonly used by men to gain a following. Instead He reveals Himself to His children as wholly worthy of love and utmost confidence. Oh, that we could see that as a Father He is intimately *with* each of His sons in the time of adversity and through the hours of child-training. What a revelation! Only the so-great love of Our heavenly Father could subject a son to this extreme crucible of suffering. As human fathers we know only too well how prone we are to spare those we love. Often, in doing so we

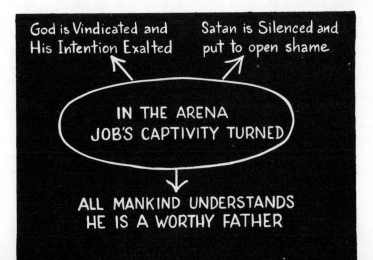

really are only sparing ourselves.

It would seem that only one of very special worth and value to God in His plan would be subjected to open display before all the eyes of eternity. Yet one who has taken his place with Christ in the heavenlies realizes that Job's case is not unique. The very nature and character of THE FATHER requires that all His sons shall be tried — all must have their captivity turned ere they can fully know Him as the Father.

JOB'S GREATEST NEED

The story of Job has been used to illustrate almost every conceivable Christian experience or condition. Some insist that Job needed salvation, others say his need was healing. Others point to the needs of detachment from possessions, or patience in suffering. The story does reveal these needs as a part of Job's experience. But there is something basic to be learned from these common interpretations of Job's predicament; and that is: men always are (like Job) far more conscious of Job (themselves) than they are of God. Preachers and teachers do not usually emphasize what *God intended to realize through Job,* but rather what Job needed God to do *for him.* Let no one assume he is wholly rectified in his philosophy or purpose while he is still centered in self, and using God for his own blessing and benefit. We cannot escape revealing ourselves and where we place the priority. Speech and action testify whether it is with God or man.

The turning of Job's captivity reveals something of a pattern. In a sense, God placed Job in this crucible experience to show what kind of ultimate rectification must be accomplished in us, if we are to realize His ultimate intention. It seems quite evident that at the beginning of the story Job had not yet chosen the way of the inwrought Cross and was not centered in God and His way of life.

Throughout the entire trial every circumstance pointed to one grand climax. As we move through chapter after chapter, the nature of Job's problem becomes more clear. In chapter twenty-nine Job's trouble is pin-pointed by the Holy Spirit. He is found using the personal pronoun forty-eight times in the chapter's twenty-five verses. This is the old self-relating philosophy of Adam. Job was utterly blind to his deepest need. He saw himself only as one *who tried so hard* to please God. But this was the trouble; he was still the center.

As we reach the last chapter of the book, Job has moved from the place of "hearing about" to the place of "seeing" God. He has confessed his rashness and repented in dust and ashes. Suddenly we reach the full disclosure of how all these experiences have led up to one thing:

"THE LORD TURNED THE CAPTIVITY OF JOB"

Behold! Here is a man who was rectified at the very mainspring of his life. Thus did God perform that which was appointed for Job. But note! It is not written that the Lord turned the captivity of Job and *then* he prayed for his friends. This is always man's way of reasoning. But the Bible tells us he prayed for his friends, *then* his own release came. God had so changed Job's point of view that his heart responded when his friends called for prayer. No longer wrapped in the mantle of his own despair, Job was able to understand the needs of others. Once it would have seemed to Job that his first concern was prayer for himself; now, he could see others. The Lord said nothing to Job of deliverance for himself. Instead He sent back the "comforters" so he could pray for those who had spoken of him so spitefully.

Bidden of God, the three men went for prayer to the outcast upon the ash heap. Job prayed for them, and as he did, the word of authority was spoken from the throne. Job had become a fit container in which God could, through the working of death, bring forth life for others. He seemed to select His favorite among men to demonstrate how all have "fallen short of the glory of God," or as Fenton translated it: "All are in need of rectification from God" (Rom. 3:23).

It was not enough to bring a proud, self-relating man into the dust. God must also give him a full vision, a philosophy of life, which would bring him into full harmony with the Father and His intention. Job was rectified! Of that we are sure. How else could he pray sincerely for friends who have misjudged him cruelly and spoken to him harshly? Although he had not yet been vindicated by deliverance, there was no rancor. Could a thread of self-concern have lurked in his heart to whisper that God might bless these apparently undeserving friends while leaving him bereft? Did he wonder what they might think concerning his continued testing? Did he suspicion that even as he prayed they might be mocking him?

That Job was rectified, that the inwrought Cross had begun its work, is to be seen in the fact that God heard Job's prayer. As Job prayed, the word of authority was spoken from the throne. God seemed to say, "Deliver my servant Job, I have already realized my ultimate intention of rectification in him. Now I can accomplish an outward deliverance." Thus the kingly soul, already free of inward bondage, was now set free from the bonds of affliction. The latter days of his fruitfulness unto God were much greater than the first. The Father could now dare to share with him all that He knew could be rightly used in realizing His intention.

Many would like to know more about the subjective workings of Job's restoration. But of these we are not told. Possibly they are of little importance in the eyes of the Lord who looks upon the heart. It may be the all-wise Father knew how others of His children, when in the furnace of trial, would be tempted to set their minds on visible signs of restoration, rather than on the *turning of captivity*, which is to Him of much greater value.

Even at this point we may miss the focus of Job's rectification. If we are still mostly interested in the benefits which Job received, we have not yet come alive to God and what will satisfy Him. The rectifying point in Job's trial came when he moved over into God and His concern. He adopted the poured out manner of life that will always bring deliverance to others. It is in this position of self-forgetfulness that the greatest deliverances come.

T. A. Sparks shares this testimony:

You can become tied up with your own spiritual problems.... The way out is to have the burden of all God's people on your heart. That creates ministry, that means strength, that means praying. It is an emancipating thing to have the Lord's burden. Have you got it, or are you dabbling with things, toying with pebbles on the beach instead of being out in the deep with God in His big things? Are you just interested, or desperately concerned; just having a nice pleasant time, or really carrying God's need in His people on your heart?

In the next lesson it is our purpose to see another chosen vessel of the Lord whose complete rectification made him long to see the Church so rectified.

Further study on captivity turned can be pursued in these Scripture portions: Eph. 4:8; Psa. 68:18; 2 Cor. 10:5; Rom. 7:23; Zeph. 3:20; Hos. 6:11; Job 42:11 and Jer. 29:14.

HOW THRILLING it is to live in the larger viewpoint and have the Father explain what He is accomplishing now in this present age. In His plan of sanctification we see how He deliberately follows a pattern. Just as the husbandman plants one seed that he might have a harvest of much fruit after its kind, so the eternal Father plants His precious Son that He might in due time bring many sons to glory. How often we have become so fascinated with the growth of the grain that we have overlooked the Husbandman and His intention in . . .

The Planting and the Harvest

A WONDERFUL, though seldom detected, theme runs through the book of Hebrews. Briefly, it is the story of two bodies the Father has designed for His Son. As a Husbandman, the Father planted His only begotten Son and waits for the growth and harvest of many sons who will one day come to glory. God has spoken His full and all-inclusive message by this Son and He will continue to speak throughout the whole universe in ages to come by His coming (corporate) Son. A summary of this theme as it is to be seen as follows:

THE SON . . . "God hath . . . spoken . . . in His Son" (literally, son-wise) (1:2).

"Thou art my Son . . ." (1:5).

"But of the Son He saith . . ." (1:8).

"Christ as Son over his (God's house . . .). (3:6).

The Sons... "bringing many sons unto glory." (2:10).

"My son, regard not lightly...the chastening..." (12:5).

"...every son whom He receiveth..." (12:6).

"God dealeth with you as with sons..." (12:7).

"Ye are come to the church (assembly) of the First-born who are registered [as citizens] in heaven." (12:23, A.N.T.).

Here are two bodies: "...when He (Christ) entered into the world, He said...you have made ready a body for Me [to offer]" (Heb. 10:5, A.N.T.). This natural body which He received was offered (planted) in death. But there is another Body of which Paul speaks in Colossians 1:18 which is the many-membered Body — the Church.

God's Word speaks much of the first body which the Lord Jesus sacrificed on the Cross that we might experience a personal setting apart unto God (Heb. 10:10). But here we have only the foothills of truth. The summit of truth reaches far up into a corporate experience of which we only have glimpses at present. "Till we all come... unto a perfect man," Paul wrote, "unto the measure of the stature of the fulness of Christ" (Eph. 4:13). Not unto perfect men, but one perfect man—all of us together, Head and Body—a perfect man. "For as the body is one, and hath many members and all the members of that one body, being many, are one body: so also is Christ" (1 Cor. 12:12). Norman Grubb notes that it does not say, "so also is the *body* of Christ," but "so also is Christ." Can we conceive of this? We are led to a final unification with Christ which is beyond our present understanding. When the Father fulfills the mystery of His will, He will gather together "in one all things in Christ, both which are in heaven and which are on earth" (Eph. 1:10).

We have barest glimpses of future glories. Perhaps some of these truths were contained in the "unspeakable words" which Paul heard, but was not permitted to utter. Even though there is much we have not been told, the truths revealed take us from the marvelous truth of *Christ in us* to the even more wonderful revelation of *us in Christ*. Who can measure the implications of this?

However, we are not left in the dark concerning one fact: God's vision is not centered so much on the individual, as on the Church; nor are His mighty works done through the single member, but through the Body. Why then, we may ask, do we spend so much time searching into our individual relationship of Him? Why did Jesus and those who followed Him show utmost concern for individuals? Because as was said of Soren Kierkegaard:

When he spoke to the individual, calling him to seek purity of heart and integrity of will, he was doing the thing he believed best calculated to fit men to act as a responsible community. If he spoke more of the individual than of the community, it was because the first thing necessary was to restore the true individuality without which true community is not possible. Individuality, not individualism, was his primary aim.

Through inner integration—that holiness which is wholeness—we are liberated from self-centeredness in order that the Head of the Body can share with us His body-consciousness. Here we must observe real caution. It is possible to talk the language of external unity while building on foundations of sand. The truth of the Vine-branch relationship must be an individual experience before the believer can participate in the wider corporate implications.

It seems in the present hour that men are victims of two extremes. One group emphasizes bringing individuals to Christ. The tremendous emphasis placed by the New Testament writers on the relationship of the individual to Christ justifies us in doing the same; but we must not stop there. We must move on to see individual integration into the Body. Others become overanxious to explore the ways to external unity without first being concerned with the spiritual condition of individuals thus united. This is the other extreme. God's intention is clear: When people are living in union with Christ, they are also in living union with one another.

HOW LIFE-UNION BEGINS

Now let us see God's method for placing us into His Body. Consider this perfect Seed, the Lord Jesus, for whom the Father prepared a body. Surely Jesus knew the purpose of the Father in His being planted. When certain Greeks came and asked to see Jesus, His answer was amazing to some, and many have missed its significance. What was His reason for saying, "Verily, I say unto you, except a corn of wheat fall into the ground and die, it abideth alone: but if it die, it bringeth forth much fruit" (John 12:24)?

I understand the meaning to be simply this: for these Gentiles, the corn of wheat must first fall into the ground and die—"Christ must be lifted up on the Cross and believed in as a sacrifice for sin as Seed of Abraham, not David" (C.I. Scofield). The hour would yet come when Gentiles would be privileged to see THE CHRIST—as a many-membered Body. Now as the Son (in a singular sense) He was not yet to be made known to them. The Gentile world will know Him when He comes as the Head united with His Body—the Church. And not until the time of the manifestation of the many sons—the "much fruit"—will Gentiles fully grasp the truth and appreciate THE CHRIST.

THE SON IS PLANTED

When we look more closely at what God is doing in this present age, we are amazed at our slowness to understand the truths concerning the Body which He is preparing. In the Gospel of Mark, Jesus gives a clear picture of what happens to THE SEED which the Father has planted in the earth. Out of death will spring resurrection life: "first the blade, then the ear, and after that the full corn in the ear" (Mk. 4:28). Of course one can visualize this as the growth process of every individual, but we are primarily concerned here with the corporate Body. We see the Early Church as the blade. Since that day nearly 2,000 years ago, when it sprang forth in newness of life the Church has grown to the ear stage, and we believe it will soon mature to become the "full corn in the ear." The harvest is about to come. It seems there are yet many kernels unripened and unprepared for the Husbandman's sickle.

It will help us much if we come to understand God's sanctifying work throughout this dispensation. The infant Church which began as a blade was wonderful to behold. How many have wished to return to that first-century life-practice as recorded in the book of Acts. We must be careful to recognize what was there in blade stage is finally coming to a more glorious full-ear stage. So we err when we attempt only to imitate the Early Church in its form. God is interested today in the spontaneous expression of the life of the Lord Jesus, which is the same both in principle and practice as it was in the springing up of the Church. But the mature, full-ear corn is different from the tender blade.

It will be helpful to see that God's sanctifying method by which He brings the blade to full corn in the ear consists of *crisis, process* and *goal*. Sanctification in the personal experience is often a crisis which brings tremendous conflict. This is primarily because the gospel has not been preached in its fulness; and souls converted under such circumstances have not had an adequate experience of salvation. They were not from the beginning aware of all they were to be delivered from, of the life they were delivered to, nor of all the means by which full realization of God's intention is to be brought about.

Where the Gospel is proclaimed in fulness and Christ is presented as Saviour and sovereign Lord, the initial surrender to Him is so complete that the crisis phase of sanctification is scarcely felt. The

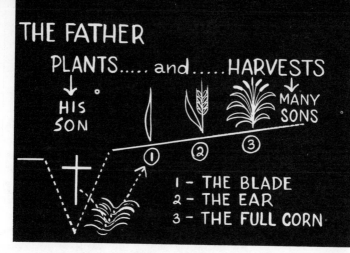

THE FATHER
PLANTS..... and .....HARVESTS
HIS SON ↓
MANY SONS ↓
1 - THE BLADE
2 - THE EAR
3 - THE FULL CORN

process begins from the first moment of the new life. This is as it should be in every life. But even so, it is only as objective truth becomes subjective that sanctification develops. It (sanctification) must take place, whether in one blazing experience at conversion, or through painful steps of separation along the way, or later in one revolutionary crisis as the truth dawns in fulness.

Now what is true of the individual is also true of every group which exists as a corporate expression of Christ's life. Whenever a local church has been founded on the fuller message of God's sovereignty and holiness, it avoids the need for later crisis of separation and detachment. But separation must come before any church can be a worthy expression of the Lord. Oh, how many hurts and divisions could be prevented if God's full-orbed message were presented from the beginning.

The blade must undergo such scorching winds and dry seasons that it would seem almost to wither. Yet this is God's way of bringing it to maturity and the production of the full corn in the ear. We have been brought into a corporate union *(the crisis)* which has this marvelous *goal* in view. But we often overlook what constitutes the *process* of development between the beginning blade and the mature corn.

We have pointed out that separation—sanctification—is the necessary process of growth. There is, of course, the positional sanctification which means we are "in Christ." Paul addresses the Corinthian church as "Them that are sanctified in Christ Jesus, called saints." This is the objective truth. It is presented in order that faith may lay hold of it, and that we, entering into it's truth by the gracious activity of the Holy Spirit, may become in experience what we are by faith. As C. H. McIntosh explains, "The more clearly we enter by faith into objective truth, or what is true of us in Christ, the deeper, more experimental, and practical, will be the subjective work in us, and the more complete will be the exhibition of the moral effect in our life and character." In response to our faith, the Holy Spirit makes the truth real to our hearts and enables us to make it true also in our lives.

The words "sanctification" and "holiness" are practically interchangeable. They both have the twofold thought of "purification from" and "separation to." The terms are backward and forward looks at the same vein of truth. We make a great mistake if we limit either word to mean purification from sin. That which is purified is also separated to God in order that it may be a glorious vessel for the manifestation of Christ's glory. Sanctification (holiness) always has this goal in view. Our obedience to the heavenly vision of what God intends, brings the powers of heaven down to earth, to make the believer heavenly in nature, in disposition, in character, in conduct. Thus Christ is manifested in individuals, now in a measure, as He is to be made manifest in fulness through His Church in ages to come.

A THREE-FOLD PROCESS

How does the Holy Spirit work in this body? The process is a simple, though often a painful one. He illumines the heart of the believer, reveals the truth, and enables us to translate it into life. He becomes "the spirit of wisdom and revelation in the knowledge of Christ." The process of sanctification may then be summed up in three words: REVELATION, APPROPRIATION, and ACTUALIZATION. The Holy Spirit unveils the truth, that is *revelation;* the child responds in an energized working of appropriating faith; so the truth becomes actual in experience. This process is going on all the time, for it is a series of progressive unfoldings and realizations. As in the individual life of the believer, and in the corporate history of each local congregation, so in history the Church has been moving from blade, to ear, and unto full-corn maturity.

We shall see in a coming lesson that Paul seemed to realize that no true measure of maturity would ever come until the Church had her captivity turned. Through the centuries she has been mostly inverted, living unto what she might receive from her Lord; but wholly indifferent to what she, as a corporate Body, might be unto Him. Once this has been made clear, the sanctifying process becomes for her a continual choice between those things that are merely *for her* or for the life that is *unto Him.* She begins to live by the heavenly philosophy and rule of life.

Somehow we are moved with the deepest conviction that, while individual members have been caught by the revelation of living unto THE HEAD, surely the hour of crisis is at hand when God will use persecution and pressure to bring the *Church as a Body* to that revelation. Her captivity must be turned before she will turn from ease, pleasure and the glory of her own accomplishments. Until her captivity is turned, she will never cease from programming, and building costly monuments to her own honor.

The time for the awakening to divine purpose has come. There is no other way to explain the intensifying discipline of so many of the Lord's people in this present hour. Suffering abounds on every hand. This will surely increase until the Body enters into universal travail. The Church must suffer pangs of labor in order to bring forth a new day. Nothing makes us so body-conscious as suffering. There is something wonderful about the sympathetic vibration which flows through the body, as one member suffers the whole body suffers. This is true of the natural body and it is true of the Church.

THE LATTER RAIN WAS FOR RIPENING

Perhaps a look at conditions governing seedtime and harvest in Palestine might enable us to understand the growth of the Church. First, observe that the oriental seedtime is preceded by a copious rainfall called the "early rain." This softens the hard, heated earth to prepare it for sowing. The grain springs up quickly and continues to grow for several months, then it suddenly seems to come to a standstill. Maturity and ripening depend on the "latter rain." If rain is long delayed the stalks grow yellow; and the ear, if seen at all, presents a dry, shriveled appearance. No wonder the husbandman anxiously waits for the rain, constantly watching the distant horizon for the first indication of gathering clouds which will bring the longed for showers.

Undoubtedly the "early rain" in a figurative sense was the outpouring of the Holy Spirit on the day of Pentecost. From this first refreshing rain the young blade got a good start. Then, as in the natural realm, there is a period when the grain puts forth no apparent growth, but seems to stand still; so has been the growth of the body. As the Holy Spirit was less recognized and obeyed there came a declension. Growth became less marked. While the natural rain does not cease during the middle season of growth, only enough falls to keep it alive. The Church has had its intermittent showers to keep it alive through the centuries.

Now there is expectancy on every hand. The hour has come when the latter rain is needed to bring the great harvest to fruition. The Husbandman has had long patience in waiting for the time of the latter rain and the maturity of His harvest. He is saying to His children now:

"Ask ye the Lord rain in the time of the latter rain; so the Lord shall make bright clouds and give them showers of rain" (Zech. 10:1).

Evidently God's people are awakening to their need of maturity. An increasing sense of pressure, helplessness and failure has taken possession of them, and throughout the world one hears the groaning for grain-ripening rain. The harvest of God's planting will mature, but the individual kernel does not reach that maturity by living with a primary concern for its own welfare and growth. God's way is just the opposite. Real maturity and fruitfulness unto God is always manifest in a sharing of God's concern for the growth of others. Self-concern and self-saving is the way of spiritual death. As was true with God's Son, so it will be true with every "corn of wheat" who would be fruitful.

"There is no gain but by a loss;
You cannot save but by a cross.
The corn of wheat, to multiply,
Must fall into the ground and die.
Wherever you ripe fields behold,
Waving to God their sheaves of gold,
Be sure some corn of wheat has died,
Some soul has there been crucified;
Someone has wrestled, wept and prayed,
And fought hell's legions undismayed."

—Selected.

THE CLOSER WE COME to the hour when the Father
will unveil His many sons before all the universe, the
more breathless becomes our anticipation. Too long has
our attention been centered upon the glory which we
will personally receive. Now as we behold the mystery
of the Christ, the corporate body, unfolded before our
eyes, we are thrilled with the glory He will receive.
The more we grasp of the Father's intention the more
we see the transcendence and . . .

The Glory of Sonship

TO UNDERSTAND THE BIBLICAL conception of adoption and
sonship, we must first have some background to show how oriental
customs in this regard differ from our Western concepts.

In Eastern lands it was the practice of a noble-father to submit his
infant male child to the child-training and tutelage of a trusted household servant. This was possible because many slaves were captives
from conquered civilized nations. Educated, noble in character, and
qualified to serve as pedagogue or child-trainer, such slaves were
esteemed members of the household staff. It was into such custody
that the infant child was entrusted until the time when he should
come of age.

Actually then, the child, though heir apparent, was no different from
the servant to whom he must submit. During the long period of child-
training it was the tutor's task to bring the child into the ways, pur-

poses, and spirit of the father of the family. Finally when the child became fourteen or sixteen years of age, it was the custom to hold a formal celebration for his coming out. Thus the child, who had been waiting with anticipation for this day appointed by his father, was presented to the household, host of friends, and family. This ceremony, called adoption, meant the coming of a son to his full rights in the family.

From this we gain a better understanding of the four ascending steps we have pictured on the blackboard. We see: (1) the ministry of the Spirit; (2) the meaning of Bible adoption; (3) the Father's intention in the unveiling, and (4) the glory of sonship. When we see how most of Christendom has missed the larger intention of the Holy Spirit's coming and ministry, we understand how imperative it is to live in the PATERNAL OUTLOOK. Only then do we see how Fatherhood is the key to understanding God's purposes for the Son and His many sons.

THE MINISTRY OF THE SPIRIT

Too often it seems the blessed Holy Spirit is looked upon as little more than "a blessing machine." To assume He has been sent primarily for our benefit and comfort is to miss the Father's intention. It is the Spirit who actualizes the believer's sonship. "... God hath sent forth the Spirit of His Son into your hearts, crying **Abba,** Father" (Gal. 4:6). So what the law did as child-trainer for Israel, the Spirit of adoption is to accomplish for us. We have been given an indwelling Teacher in order that the Father's intention of bringing us to full-sonship be realized. This makes clear the need for the Spirit's government. When, by faith, we take the position of full committal to the Lordship of Christ, the Holy Spirit will begin to do things in our lives and in our circumstances that will raise practical issues of obedience. No father could ever be satisfied that, in the truest sense, he had embodied himself in his son until that son had imbibed his very spirit, purpose and dedication. So the heavenly Father has placed all his natural sons under the tutelage of the law as a means of revealing to them their short comings. But sons born into His family are given the Spirit as a Teacher to bring them into full sonship.

THE MEANING OF BIBLE ADOPTION

Wherein does a son differ from a child? Adoption makes the difference. In the West, adoption is the taking of a child from one family and making it a member of another. The Greek or Roman father, however, adopted none as a son but his own child. Birth made him a child, adoption gave him sonship. Between birth and adoption there was growth, education and discipline.

At this present hour we who are born-ones (teknon) are learning to walk after the Spirit. Thus the Spirit of adoption working within is leading us more and more into the reality of sonship. But for the actual "placing of sons" (huiothesia) we are still eagerly waiting. R. B. Jones, English writer, clarifies this:

To be a son is infinitely more than to be a child, and the terms are never loosely used by the Holy Spirit. It is not a difference in relationship, but in position. Every "born again" child of God has in him the nature of His Father, and is a beloved member of His Father's family. Adoption cannot make the child any nearer or dearer, yet it gives the child a status he did not enjoy before, a position he did not occupy. It is his recognition as an adult son, the attaining of his majority, the seal upon his growth to maturity of mind and character. A child is one born of God; a son is one taught of God. A child has God's nature; a son has God's character.

It will be remembered that in earlier lessons we referred to sonship, heirship and throneship. For the sake of simplicity, in the early chapters we have used the term sonship, but only in a sense is that accurate. God's idea is that of ultimate sonship. This involves, as we see, much more than being born into the family; it is rather the full attainment of responsibility which comes to those who have arrived at maturity. We remember that Isaiah, hundreds of years before Christ, points by the Spirit to this precious truth:

"Unto us a child is born, Unto us a son is given.
And the government shall be upon His shoulder."
                                        —Isaiah 9:6

The prophet was of course speaking of the Lord Jesus. In due time the hour came when a child was born in Bethlehem's manger. He was finally recognized openly by the Father at Jordan as the heavens opened and John heard Him say, "This is my beloved Son in whom I am well pleased."

There He was given—revealed to full-sonship rights—to all who would receive Him. What a delight He was to the Father. If earthly fathers long for their offspring to imbibe their spirit, mind, heart, purpose and dedication, how much greater is the longing of our heavenly Father that we might come to fully share His Spirit, mind, heart, purpose and dedication. We now have the Firstfruit of the Spirit—we have Him, but how much does He have of us? We remember that the Spirit was

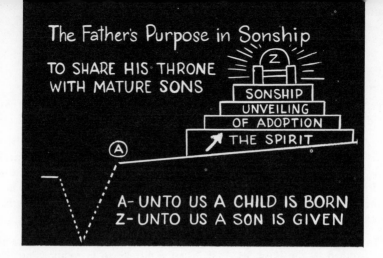

The Father's Purpose in Sonship

TO SHARE HIS THRONE
WITH MATURE SONS

Z

SONSHIP
UNVEILING
OF ADOPTION
THE SPIRIT

(A)

A- UNTO US A CHILD IS BORN
Z- UNTO US A SON IS GIVEN

poured out without measure upon Jesus. To what measure have we received Him?

OUR PRESENTATION – THEN OUR UNVEILING

We are now waiting! As His own begotten ones we are waiting for the return of our Lord in the air when we shall be caught away to be presented before Him "without spot or wrinkle or any such thing." Such is the hope that should purify us!

Yet not only do we hope and wait, but the rest of creation is also waiting as in a sort of universal travail. Waiting—not to be caught away, but for deliverance which shall come when we have returned from the "bema" seat of Christ; it is a groaning and thus waiting for the manifestation of the sons of God, a waiting for the day of adoption or unveiling which will signal its deliverance from the curse. Yes, it is in that glorious day of unveiling that the Father will display to a wondering universe His Son and sons. In that day we will be ready with the Lord Jesus to share in the government which shall be upon His shoulder (Rom. 8:19-25; Eph. 3:10-11; 5:27.) J. B. Phillips has so well portrayed this in Romans 8:18:

"In my opinion whatever we may have to go through now is less than nothing compared with the magnificent future God has planned for us. The whole creation is on tip-toe to see the wonderful sight of the sons of God coming into their own."

What could be more wonderful than to realize that we have been predestined "unto the adoption of sons by Jesus Christ to Himself" (Eph. 1:5). The word "children" in the Authorized Version is out of harmony with Paul's idea of adoption, and so is the preposition "of." The Greek word "huiothesia," denoting "sonship," is used instead of "children." "Adoption of children" is acceptable to the English mind, where we think of children as the subjects of adoption. But Paul is speaking of "born ones" who are destined to a place of full maturity, responsibility, and authority in the family of God.

Paul had the ear of a poet and a seer. "We know," he says, "that all creation groaneth and travaileth." He sees nature as unsatisfied— The thunders are complaining, the rolling years are moaning, the winds are wailing, and the flowers are withering. Something must happen.

"For (even the whole) creation (all nature) waits expectantly *and* longs earnestly for God's sons to be made known — waits for the revealing, the disclosing of their sonship " (Rom. 8:19 A.N.T.)

Creation here can only mean the world of nature. It cannot mean the sons of God, for they are that which is awaited. It cannot mean the evil world system, because none of it will share in the glory. It cannot mean the angels, because they are not described in the creation story. There is only one possible meaning. It is this: the physical, material world of plants, animals and earth which God has made as the habitation of His family, groans and suffers along with us under a condition of mortality and corruption.

Not only so! "...we ourselves, who have the first fruits of the Spirit, are groaning within ourselves, waiting for the adoption" (the placing in full sonship). For while we know we are God's children, we are waiting for the son's robe. Our robes are now ragged. This corruptible body is not good enough for sons, we are waiting for the redemption of the body. Until sonship is complete we rejoice to be in the family; and while we are able to say "Hallelujah," there is ever another cry, "Even so, come (quickly) Lord Jesus."

The J. B. Phillips version says, *"It is plain to anyone with eyes to see that at the present time all created life groans in a sort of universal travail. And it is plain, too, that we who have the foretaste of the Spirit are in a state of tension, while we wait for that redemption of our bodies which will at last mean we have REALIZED OUR FULL SONSHIP IN HIM"* (Rom. 8:23).

THE GLORY OF SONSHIP

You will agree, when you survey the whole of Christendom today, that there are very few believers who have light or revelation concerning the Body of Christ or the calling to full-sonship. The adversary has used every blinding, darkening, withholding and devisive effort to keep us from the light of the Church's true nature, calling and destiny. We must see that this is not an optional truth which we may look into if time permits, but it is truth central to the very purpose of realizing a temple for His glory. How many believers have gotten a glimpse of some glory *they* will receive, but have been blinded to living *only unto His glory*.

Graduation from the school of sonship will be to the throne. It was this which the noble-father had in view as he awaited the "huiothesia" of his son. For this was the day when the father began to share his authority and government with his son. For this reason our Father has waited while the Holy Spirit "leads us into all truth." In His school room we pass through spiritual infancy and childhood, where everything is done *for us*, into a place where God's purpose can be accomplished *through us*. When we graduate from this school it will be *together* as a class. As one new man we will reach the time of adoption as a corporate body. This is disappointing to those who have a selfish itch to get ahead or to be recognized as "greatest," but God's concern is with the body. Once we have become body-conscious we will begin to live unto Him in achieving maturity in the Church. We will forget about our own attainment and become occupied with the attainment of others.

Romans 8 presents these four aspects of sonship: (1) We receive and walk in the Spirit (Rom. 8:14, 16). (2) The Spirit of adoption comes to us as the child-trainer (8:15). (2) We await the unveiling or manifestation of the sons of God (8:19). (4) Full-sonship or adoption comes when we receive our heavenly house from above (8:23).

IT WOULD BE IMPOSSIBLE to be seated, as we have, in the eternal viewpoint of our Father, and be indifferent to His time-clock and the progress of history as it nears its end. Like players at chess, we can see how every move of world leaders is rapidly forcing the crisis of the ages. Stalemate here, check there — the struggle between two governments is about over. In this chapter it is imperative that all who have spiritual discernment recognize . . .

The Pressing Issue of this Hour

GOD IS NOW DOING a very special thing in those of His people who are pressing on with Him with marked purposefulness. There is a sweeping and terrible battle raging for the throne of this world. A greater warfare has never been known. The enemy is marshalling all his power and all his puppets in vivid array. There is an urgent summons for the people of God to recognize the challenge. Who will take the government of the universe?

Unless men have spiritual discernment to see what is behind the present world situation, they will not rise to the challenge of the enemy. God's sons are being prepared and called to take the kingdom *now*, in a spiritual way, in order that they may share the throne in the age to come.

There is a reason why the enemy is determined to keep truth concerning the body of Christ from the Lord's people. Any group which constitutes such an expression of truth will become the target for Satan's heaviest onslaughts from every side. We all know the value of a fearless individual's testimony to truth. How much greater, then, would be the concerted power of a corporate body, testifying to the world that God's children can fellowship in perfect harmony. When the Church is one, then shall the world believe.

"So that they all may be one [just] as You, Father, are in Me and I in You, that they also may be one in Us, so that the world may believe and be convinced that You have sent Me" (John 17:21, A.N.T.).

God's Word says "one shall chase a thousand, but two shall put ten thousand to flight." There is strength in unity. Satan understands that he will be immediately deposed when the corporate Son comes into full manifestation, for then he will lose his position and his hold. The issue which was settled at Calvary will be finally enforced, for ever since the Lord openly triumphed on the Cross, the enemy has been governmentally judged and put to shame. He rules only because man has not forced the issue upon him, but has instead sided with him or compromised with his rule. This is, in a fashion, like the anarchy that occurs when the president of a country cannot bring the rest of the government to stand with him in enforcing edicts which are already constitutionally decided. Christ has triumphed, but His people have not yet stood with Him in victory.

As some may have already discerned, the more God's corporate Son rises in the Spirit to a place of authority, the more vicious become the onslaughts of the enemy in the spiritual realm. As soon as the corporate Son is manifested in glory—as soon as he stands on his feet and is united in every respect with the Head—the enemy will be cast down from the heavenlies and will wage warfare in awful fury in the earth.

The warfare of the Church has always been a spiritual warfare.

THE PRESSING ISSUE of this HOUR !

③

OF THE INCREASE OF HIS GOVERNMENT THERE SHALL BE NO END

②

①   ↓   ↓

TOTALITARIAN	ANARCHY	THEOCRACY
Is imposed rule without considering Moral Rights.	Is attempt to keep one's rights in the Exercise of Self Government.	Is when all rights are yielded to God Who then rules through His representatives

Victory in the spiritual realm will be the cause of the time of terrible wrath and tribulation that is to proceed the final victory of the Son. Because of Satan's fury in the earth, warfare will enter (to a far greater extent) the physical and natural realm. (Rev. 12:9, 12).

To many it will seem that the great warfare in the earth now rages between communism and capitalism. This is only a surface issue. If we would understand the real spiritual conflict we must: (1) recognize the foundation and structure of government, (2) discern the fundamental concepts of government, and (3) understand God's ultimate intention in world government.

THE FOUNDATION OF GOVERNMENT

There are two fundamental concepts of government and human rights. (1) There have long been those who recognize that the source of all authority is God. Man, therefore, because he is in the image and likeness of God, is endowed with certain inalienable rights; (2) others hold that the source of all rights is inherently invested in government. These two concepts are best illustrated by the constitutions of the United States and the Soviet Union. The founding fathers of our country recognized God's authority when they wrote in the second paragraph of our constitution recognition that all men are "endowed by their Creator with certain inalienable rights—life, liberty, and the pursuit of happiness."

Now by contrast, under a totalitarian system such as the Soviet constitution provides, all rights are bestowed by the state. Note the difference! If rights come to us from God, then no state, no parliament, no dictator can take them away (except by God's permission, as in punishment for misuse). If it is true, however, that they are granted by the state, then the state can take them away.

In the Soviet constitution, you go through nine chapters, 117 articles, which set up an absolute, totalitarian, monolithic, materialistic state, before you come to the mention of a single right. After waiting all this time, and wading through all this communist double talk, you are naturally full of expectancy to find what rights are provided to the people. What do you think the first one is? The right to work! Not even the right to life. All the half-dozen rights of the people are guaranteed by the state.

This reveals one fundamental difference. Either the state exists for the person (as in our country), or the person for the state (as in the Soviet). In America, the person has rights independent of the state; in the Soviet, no rights are inalienable; they may all be taken away by the state that gave them. Thus the state usurps the place of God. Sovietism is virtual atheism.

Karl Marx understood the inherent source of rights even better than some Americans. He did not like democracy because he said it is founded on the principle that every man has a soul, independent of any social order or class. Marx said, "I contend that only the class has rights. An individual has no value whatsoever unless he is a member of the revolutionary class."

We understand this difference between the person and the class: A person is a being with a rational soul, and therefore has rights. A pig has no rational soul (only animal instincts and appetites), therefore no rights. Likewise a flower has no soul and therefore has no rights. In the Soviet, however, men, like pigs or flowers, are used or plucked at will by the state who controls them. They are seen only as they appear in blocs or classes. Individuals have no rights, but a class has power useful to the state.

FUNDAMENTAL CONCEPTS OF GOVERNMENT

On the blackboard we have illustrated the three fundamental types of government which issue out of God's order of things. They are theocracy, anarchy and totalitarianism.

In order to understand government, we must return to a proper starting point in God. When we recognize that God, who is the ultimate source of rights, has designed that man should be only a proximate source of rights, we can understand what happened to Adam in the garden. According to God's design, Adam was to have yielded all his rights to God, thereby allowing God to rule through him as a vice-regent in the earth. Had Adam and his posterity followed this plan, it would have meant theocracy—the wonderful government of God over all the universe. Instead Adam chose to keep the rights for himself. Governed by his appetite he entered upon a course of self-rule which actually brought anarchy. He wanted to be a god in his own right—free to do that which seemed right in his own eyes. This in essence is the spirit of anarchy which has ruled in rebellious hearts since the Fall.

As we have said before, the neutral plane in government is only a passing zone. Man must come under the government of God, for in the attempt to be wholly free, he will fall under the bondage of totalitarian rule—first in bondage to his appetites, then as slave to Satan. The devil who gained the dictatorship over Adam, will also rule Adam's sons.

If we are honest enough to face the full implications of this principle, we will see that democracy can work only as long as men deliberately choose God as their individual ruler and submit themselves and their rights to Him. As God is allowed to set up a theocracy over individual lives of a people, they are able to maintain freedom from oppression.

Now let us see what has happened to our democracy. Because of the utter selfishness of men, our citizens have insisted on using their rights for their own welfare and benefit. The spiritually dead are alive only to appetite. Instead of living unto God with concern for the needs of others, each has done that which seems right in his own eyes. As a result the trend in recent years has been for government to step in to curb selfish tendencies. Although the people have not, in the constitution, given the government the right to do this, it has usurped more power to act for what it calls "the common good." The power of the class has been discovered and exploited, and our present trend toward a welfare state has the inherent seeds of totalitarianism.

It requires little wisdom to recognize that all government tends to one of these types: God-rule or self-rule or Satan-rule. The typical modern man does not really want self-rule. He only thinks he does. Self-rule implies too much responsibility, and responsibility is a burden—the awful burden of answering the searching question, "What is the real purpose of your life?" If man has a purpose, he must live purposefully. Purposeful living requires discernment and discipline. This is why theories which deny, or transfer, man's freedom are so prevalent today: "Marxism destroys freedom in terms of historical determinism, Fruedianism, dissolves freedom in the determinism of the subconscious and erotic, totalitarianism, drowns individual freedom in the collectivity of race, nation, blood or clan." (Fulton Sheen).

GOD'S ULTIMATE INTENTION IN WORLD GOVERNMENT

If men were confusing basic issues only in the political realm, it would not be so tragic; but there is the same confusion in Christ's body, the Church. To settle this confusion is the great and pressing issue of the hour. Will the Church, redeemed by His blood from bondage, live only unto herself, seeking only what He can do for her? Or will she awaken to her responsibility of living up to His ultimate intention? Only as she comes under divine authority can she truly exercise authority. It must be a total submission to the Head to live under the complete glad-hearted leadership of His Spirit.

How my heart has ached as I have witnessed in the Church those who react against the government of the Spirit, and insist upon self-rule. The basic issues of government are easily confused, for there are those who insist upon exercising their "democratic rights." Everyone has the right to vote in the local church. It is not, therefore, God who reigns, but the individual selfishness of the people. Many a church, not able to keep a pastor more than twelve or fifteen months, survives under virtual anarchy. Why? Because the pews are filled with members who know nothing of the sovereignty of God over their lives.

Of course, the opposite extreme may be seen when some strong-willed pastor ascends to the throne as virtual dictator over the people and either scatters the flock, or subjugates those who remain. He sees the need for members being conquered, but does the conquering by his own power and methods, and not in God's way through the Spirit. When men will not yield to the government of God, the totalitarian spirit will rule them by force.

The hour has come when men of judgment and wisdom must stand for divine government in the Church. To those who resist authority, this may seem to be totalitarianism. But because God has delegated His power to redeem men, He will stand with His servants even as He stood with Moses. His authority in the Church will accomplish His end in the world. We must remember that God's plan is for glad-hearted rule by those who have become His love-slaves, gladly embracing the way of the Cross. These have submitted to His government and enjoy divine rule and enter into divine purpose. Believers who submit to such government find it is not bondage, but blessedness.

However, for those who refuse rule at the hand of God and His servants and insist on the spirit of self-rule, God has arranged the imposition of moral and natural law. Law comes into play only when men step out of bounds. In all of this we can see that God is sovereign and that He must rule. But He delights only in those who with gladness of heart choose to be governed not only by the natural and moral but by the spiritual laws of His kingdom.

THE RULE OF THE SPIRIT

Did you ever see one whose body did not obey the directions of the head? We call such a disease St. Vitus's dance. It is caused by the failure of the hand or leg to respond to the impulse of the brain. This is anarchy manifest in the physical body. One glance at the spiritual body of Christ indicates this disease is hindering the Head from effectively working through His body. This condition will not prevail for long. From eternity the Father has purposed that His Son should have a body to express His life, His light and His love. Viewed from that standpoint — the standpoint of the heart of God — we see the Church will surely become the vessel unto the honor and glory which He intended. Let us consider four prepositions which explain how this ultimate intention for His Son will be attained:

(1) God has "put all things under His feet, and given him to be the head over all things to the church which is his body" (Eph. 1:22). From God's eternal viewpoint this is already accomplished. When members respond only to the Head, there will be a glorious harmony *within* the body and all shall come to the true measure of His mind, purpose, vision and Spirit.

(2) If you ever wondered why all things exist, here is Paul's explanation: "... all things were created by Him and FOR HIM" (Col. 1:16). So the Lord Jesus is not only the Head of His Body but He is to have the pre-eminence in all things. (Col. 1:18). The Father knew from the beginning the devotion and dedication of His lovely Son. The Father knew what He could expect of Him long before His supreme test at Calvary. Accordingly He chose not only to accomplish all things by Him, but *for Him*.

(3) There is a divine principle by which all things operate smoothly to the ultimate purpose. The Father designed that all shall be THROUGH HIM. It is one thing to create, but still another to perpetuate. This marks the supreme contrast between man's systems and God's rule. From eternity past it was His intention that all should have its very operation and continuance through Christ. What, therefore, is not done through Him is temporal and transitory. Only His work is eternal. "He is before all things and by (through) Him all things consist" (Col. 1:17).

(4) It is not only *in Him, for Him* and *through Him*, but *with Him* that the Father will reach out into the whole universe in the fullest expression of Himself. As the Son expresses Himself through His Body, so the Father expresses Himself through His corporate Son. So the "fulness of Him that filleth all in all" will reach out through the Body to the universe, not only in this age, but in the ages to come. Paul writes, "That in the dispensation of the fulness of times He might gather together" (or sum up) "all things in Christ" (Eph. 1:10). Yes, with Christ, as the Son of His right hand, the Father will reach out. "The government shall be upon His shoulder... and of the increase of His government and of peace there shall be no end..." (Isa. 9:6, 7).

Finally we ask, is all of this planned and intended for the only begotten Son, alone? No, God has in the pleasure of His heart designed that the entire corporate Christ will share the victory. United by His Spirit as members of His Body we are to become co-sharers in the victory and joint-reigners in the kingdom. We are included in the Father's glorious intention for His Son because we are "in Him."

"And when all things shall be subdued unto him, then shall the Son also himself be subject unto him that put all things under him, that God may be all in all" (1 Cor. 15:28).

WE HAVE BEEN carefully following the Father's program by which His children are brought to full sonship.
We have seen how every vestige of anarchy must be
dealt with before they are prepared for authority and the
throne of the universe. However, before His Body can
have any real outreach to the world and be ready for the
ULTIMATE REVELATION, one more thing is necessary.
This is the supreme evidence of the turning of captivity.
In this lesson we pick up the theme of rectification
again as we consider how He will set . . .

Love in Right Order

I HAVE ALWAYS enjoyed the love story of the Song of Solomon, but
it was not until a friend gave me the key to this book that I was able
to comprehend the hidden lesson which God would teach us from it.

The King James version fails to give the clear meaning of the fourth
verse of the first chapter. In the Latin Vulgate translation we find this:
*"He brought me into the winepress and set love in right order within
me."* Comparison with other versions confirms this as an accurate
expression of the meaning. Is it possible that this lovely book was
placed in the Bible to teach the rectification of love?

The story presents the intimate fellowship between the Bridegroom
and His bride. As we note on the blackboard it shows how the love of
the bride moves from plane to plane and is finally set in right order.

"MINE" — 2:16 or "HIS" — 7:10

In the early stages of the story the bride is filled with self-love. Love seems to her to be a one-sided relationship in which the emphasis is on *me* and *mine*. As with all love in this stage, possessiveness is the mark and undertone. In the second chapter we hear the bride give the first summary of their relationship: "My beloved is mine and I am His" (S. of Sol. 2:16).

She seems far more conscious of what He does for her, and what He gives and is to her, than she is conscious of Him. She interprets everything (including Him) as it relates to her. Alas, she soon sickens of this kind of love. Sensing this, the Bridegroom withdraws. For her own good, He must not foster her selfishness. His wisdom works a change. There is a progression and purifying of her love. She comes at last to say, "I am my beloved's and my beloved is mine" (S. of Sol. 6:3). The emphasis has changed but there is still a mixture of getting and giving. Now she is becoming more conscious of Him than of His gifts, and of what she can be to him.

After she has stood the test of love, she finally is brought to the third phase. Love is purified and set in right order. She exclaims, "I am my beloved's, and his desire is toward me!" (S. of Sol. 7:10). Here is the perfect order: "Love seeketh not its own": it is not possessive; it is alive to the other and is always joyfully giving.

The temper of love offered by a multitude of God's sons and daughters may be observed in the tenor of their prayer. Often, even twenty years after conversion, petitions still have the "my" and "mine" ring. There is still an emphasis on getting a blessing and beseeching God on the basis of self.   Many have never known, or have become insensitive to a true love-relationship in which they live for and unto God.

THREE DEGREES OF LOVE

In one of his excellent editorials Dr. A. W. Tozer, editor of *The Alliance Witness*, writes about "Three Degrees of Love." He first points out that most Christian thinkers divide love into two kinds: love based on the gratitude and love based on excellence.

The love that springs out of gratitude is found in such passages as Psalm 116:1, "I love the Lord because he hath heard my voice and my supplications," and 1 John 4:19, "We love him, because he first loved us." This is an entirely proper and legitimate kind of love and is quite acceptable to God even though it is among the most elementary and immature of the religious emotions. Love

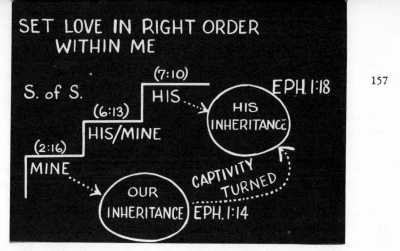

that is the result of gratitude for favors received cannot but have a certain element of selfishness in it.

This is much like the first attitude of the bride whose love is aroused, it seems, only by benefits received and does not seem to exist apart from them. But there is a higher kind of love which Dr. Tozer describes as the *love of excellence:*

This love is awakened by considerations of God's glorious being and has in it a strong element of admiration. "My beloved is white and ruddy, the chiefest among ten thousand. His mouth is most sweet; yea, he is altogether lovely" (S. of Sol. 5:10, 16). (Here then, is the second stage of the rectification of love in the bride).

This love of the divine excellencies differs from the love that springs from gratitude in that its reasons are more elevated. The element of selfishness is reduced almost to the vanishing point. We should note, however, that the two have one thing in common: they can both give a reason for their existence. Love that can offer reasons is a rational thing and has not attained to a state of complete purity. It is not perfect love.

Next, Dr. Tozer goes on to describe that highest degree of love as it must be wrought in the bride:

We must carry our love to God further than love of gratitude and love of excellence. There is an advanced stage of love whigh goes far beyond either. Down on the level of the merely human it is altogether common to find love that rises above both gratitude and admiration. The mother of a subnormal child, for instance, may love her unfortunate child with an emotional attachment altogether impossible to understand. The child excites no gratitude in her breast, for all the benefits have flowed the other way; the helpless infant has been nothing but a burden from the time it was born. Neither can the mother find in such a child any excellence to admire, for there is none.

Yet her love is something wonderful and terrible to see. Her tender feelings have swallowed the child and assimilated it to her own inward being to such a degree that she feels herself one with it....

The sum of what we say here is that there is in the higher type of love a suprarational element that cannot and does not attempt to give reasons ror its existence. It says not "I love because"; it only whispers "I love." Perfect love knows no *because*.

God in the end will work such a rectification of love in the hearts of all that are His. You will remember how He brought Job to say, "Though He slay me yet will I trust Him." There was no "because" in Job's love. Job had been brought to a place of complete surrender because he came to know who God truly is. Like Job, each of His chosen ones will belong to God with the affection that clings to Him for His sake alone. Just as God is willing to belong to man as His God *sola gratia*, by grace alone, so each member of Christ's Body will belong to God on the same basis, *for naught*. The bride must love without ulterior motive.

PAUL'S LONGING FOR THE EPHESIANS

When we realize the Church is to be prepared as a spotless bride for her Lord, we wonder if this might not be at the root of Paul's prayers in the early chapters of Ephesians. As we reach the middle of the first chapter we become keenly aware that Paul was gripped by their need, and he longs for the Spirit of God to reveal it to them. We sense the groaning in his spirit as he twice breaks forth in prayer that the Father might grant this vision to be opened to them.

In the first fourteen verses of chapter one, Paul gives a broad, panoramic background of the ultimate intention which has been in the heart of the Father from eternity. Starting with the Father, Paul reminds them of His purpose for a vast family, discloses how they have been marked out for sonship, shows how all these plans are being accomplished through the Lord Jesus, and how we receive through Him all spiritual blessings—forgiveness, acceptance, adoption, redemption and the sealing of the Holy Spirit. Paul refers to this as "our inheritance" (Ephesians 1:14).

We are not to minimize or overlook this inheritance, for the Father delights to share with His family. When man sinned He provided the death and resurrection of His Son that we might be rescued from the Fall. Yet, all God has provided for man to *receive* is not the primary concern of Paul. As he breaks forth in prayer we can catch the burden of his heart. He wants the Ephesians to have a new viewpoint. Up to this time, it seems, the Ephesians were occupied primarily with what God had done for them. They were content to camp and glory in "what is mine"—their theme was "my inheritance in Him." How much they were like the majority of believers today!

THERE IS ANOTHER INHERITANCE!

Now, in verse 18, we hear Paul begin to pray, "...that they might have the eyes of their understanding enlightened to see what is the riches of the glory of HIS INHERITANCE IN THE SAINTS."

How could these saints be brought to a concern for the Father and what He might inherit from them and through them? How could they be made alive to His interests? This is Paul's concern. In spite of all God had done *for them*, they were still inverted and man-centered. Must they continue to live as though all the universe revolved around them and existed for them? Paul discerned the need for a rectification of their love, a turning of their captivity, so they would truly live *unto God* and become His inheritance.

Recently as we drove to an evening service, a father confided to me, "The more I have given to my children, the more they want. What shall I do to help them see their selfishness?" Although he loved his family dearly, he was able to observe that they were self-centered. While they were concerned with what their father could do for them, he was concerned more with what kind of people they were growing up to be. This man had discovered a basic truth on the human level, but was only faintly aware that the heavenly Father experiences the same problem with His children. As my friend wished to jar his children from their self-centered way of looking at things, so the heavenly Father longs that His children may have a revelation of themselves, and what they are to Him.

THE WINEPRESS

How does such a revelation come? Christ's death was the basis for receiving *our inheritance*. When we recognize that we *died with Him*, then the Father begins to receive *His inheritance* as we walk in newness of life. As in Solomon's Song the Bridegroom led His bride to the winepress of frustration, sorrow and self-revelation, so He will lead each member of His corporate Body to a winepress. This is the place where He allows loved ones, circumstances and friends to inflict the deepest pain. Throughout the Scriptures the winepress is always pictured as the place where God uses the crushing instrument, the squeezing process, the pouring from vessel to vessel to bring forth the joyous wine of purified love. We are apt to relate all such experiences to the glory which shall *afterward* be ours. We may bravely, and with firmly set jaw pass through multiplied trials, never yielding to the work of love that will bring forth joy *now*. But when the true rectification of love is wrought, we become alive only to the purity and sweetness which pours forth to Him (and to those who are also His). He, oh, *He* becomes the constant center and object of our affection and attention. *His body, His* inheritance in the saints becomes central in our concern. We see clearly what Jesus meant when He said, "In as much as ye have done it unto the least of these, my brethren, ye have done it unto me." No longer is our Christian life an endurance test. It is an experience of overflowing love. Our constant prayer will be," Lord, show me how I can express this great love Thou hast brought forth within me."

Here is the fulness of rectification. When His bride truly becomes His, the Lord Jesus finds her ministering to His welfare, concerned primarily with His interests. Christ cannot deliver the kingdom to the Father, until the Church becomes alive to *His* inheritance in the saints!

Can we see it? As we center our vision on our own needs, and "try to believe God" for them, we are blind to His great love and His great purpose. When we allow Him to take us to the winepress, we discover *Him*. We find we have no other need, no other desire, than to belong only to Him — for naught.

THOUGH WE ARE coming to the close of this book, we realize in God's viewpoint that we are really reaching the commencement of that which He has ultimately intended for Himself, His Son and His family. This becomes even more evident as we observe His law of procedure: first He gives us the **miniature** in earthly form. This helps us to understand how He is working to realize the **magnitude** in heavenly reality. We shall see what this means as we observe how all things have been gradually moving toward . . .

The Glorious Ultimate Revelation

GOD DOES NOT FOREVER keep His working in secret (Deut. 29:29). It only seems to be secret because we have not had a revelation of His principles, His order and His procedure. In this chapter let us observe how those things which have their miniature in Genesis, finally come to full magnitude in the Revelation.

Consider Adam and the miniature kingdom over which man was called to reign in the Garden. One day this miniature will blossom into God's universal kingdom on earth. Observe David on the throne of Israel as a miniature of that Great David, the Lord Jesus, who will one day (with His Body) occupy the throne of the universe. Consider Solomon's beautiful temple, the earthly miniature of the glorious temple now being built of living stones to endure for eternity. Consider Adam and his bride, Eve, the miniature pre-figuration of the Lord Jesus and His bride, the Church. Consider Abraham, the father of the faithful, and remember that he is a shadow of the heavenly Father who will have an eternal family numbering as the stars of the sky and the sands of the seashore.

These are but a few of the many miniatures which will some day blossom into heavenly magnitude. In this lesson we will confine ourselves to three of these: the family, the body and the temple.

THE HOUR OF REVELATION

How glorious the day when the Lord Jesus stepped forth as the Son incarnate to reveal and glorify the Father on earth. But there were so few who caught the full significance of this manifestation of God. Even Philip, disciple of Jesus, was chided: "Have I been so long time with you Philip and you have not seen the Father; If you have seen me you have seen the Father. How is it you say, SHOW US THE FATHER?" (John 14:9).

This shows us that revelation to the hearts of men requires both truth and light. The Psalmist wrote, "O send out thy light and thy truth . . ." (Ps. 43:3). Jesus Christ stood before men as THE TRUTH, yet they needed light to shine, even upon Him, in order to realize who He was, and understand the revelation He had come to bring. As Watchman Nee puts it:

The truth is complete in Christ, but the need of our hearts is to have God's light shed on it. Apart from this—there is no revelation. All spiritual experience comes from divine light on eternal truth. Truth preached without light becomes doctrine; with divine light it becomes revelation. It always comes to us as one or the other.

When Jesus walked among men He was the Son of God only because He said it. The fact that He was the only begotten of the Father became living truth when the Holy Spirit shed light upon Him. Then He became a revelation—a window through which to behold the Father. Undoubtedly Philip had known the truth, but the light had not yet broken through to give the revelation.

Through the centuries God has allowed the revelation of Himself to break forth in hearts everywhere the Holy Spirit could make entrance in order to shed light upon truth. We marvel when we reflect on the glory which has come to the Father through every such manifestation of this First-born Son. Yet, up to this present day, how many have really known the Father? Although only a comparatively small remnant of the Church has entered into this revelation, what ecstasy and joy it

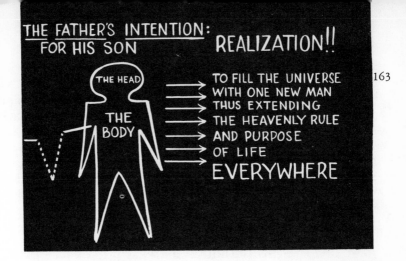

has brought to all who through the years have entered into fellowship with the Father through His Son.

But wait! There is coming a GREATER DAY of revelation. For this day all creation is waiting with bated breath. For this day of the manifestation of the sons of God, there is a deep groaning throughout all of nature. We can only faintly visualize by the eye of the Spirit what this ULTIMATE REVELATION will mean to the universe. What glory was manifest when one Son was revealed to waiting eyes! Yet, what a day when the corporate Son—Head in union with His Body, the Church—will be unveiled. The miniature caused men to cry, "Oh, Father!" What a glorious reverberation will ring throughout the corridors of heaven when the magnitude comes to be seen!

What untold splendor will be realized when the Holy Spirit pours forth light as never before upon the Head of the corporate Son. Such light will break forth upon all the universe announcing the glory of the Father, the Son and the Holy Spirit! Could Isaiah the prophet have foreseen this when he wrote,

"Arise, shine; for thy light is come, and the glory of the Lord is risen upon thee. For, behold, the darkness shall cover the earth, and gross darkness the people: but the Lord shall arise upon thee, and His glory shall be seen upon thee" (Isa. 60:1-2).

Yes, it is in this light that the whole of creation will recognize the corporate Son (each individual son conformed to the image of the First-born), and it is this which will finally bring the supreme revelation of the heavenly Father who has wrought the purpose of His heart. What a day of glory for all creation; for as one Son in that first day moved forth as the Deliverer of Zion, even so shall the many sons move as one mighty force, terrible, yet wonderful. Then shall all men know that the mighty Deliverer has come indeed, for they will witness those who have been fully delivered and brought to ultimate victory. J. B. Phillips catches the expectancy of Paul's writing as he translates Romans 8:19, "... the whole of creation is on tiptoe (waiting) to see the wonderful sight of the sons of God coming into their own. The world of creation cannot as yet see reality, not because it chooses to be blind, but because in God's purpose it has been so limited. ... "

Darkness and blindness will be no more when the Spirit of light moves once again upon the face of the deep, and the day of liberation dawns for all creation.

THE GLORIOUS MASTERPIECE

That great hour of realization is drawing near. The Father will have a family; the Son, a body; and the Spirit, a temple. It is difficult for our minds to comprehend and bring these figures together. Yet, as God's great workmanship, the Church becomes the fulfillment of His purpose for each member of the Trinity. Paul writes, "We are His workmanship," and it could well be translated, WE ARE HIS MASTER-PIECE. As the Father fashions this unique corporate Body for His Son, the habitation of the Spirit is also being framed together and growing up unto an holy temple, and this is God's family, His masterpiece of Self-revelation.

Have you ever tried to express yourself in words and been delighted to discover a short poem which expressed just what you had been laboring so hard to write in prose? How much the lovely meter and rhyme added to the expression of truth hard to express in words. It is like this with God's expression. Translators have long wished to say the word "workmanship" in Ephesians 2:10 refers to God's lovely poem. How perfectly this family will express the delight of His heart, and bring forth the pleasure and satisfaction of which He is so worthy.

Man has produced nothing which could not be improved. Only God is able to bring forth that which is perfect. Here is His *masterpiece*—even in His perfect workmanship it has no equal. We can hardly fathom the glory it will bring forth from the lips of all who behold. It will express God's LIFE through the Body, His LIGHT through the temple, and His LOVE as never known among men through the members of His family. As the divine masterpiece of the ages is unveiled, we behold in clear view the ULTIMATE GOAL to which Father, Son and Holy Spirit have been waiting to bring us.

When we look around at the discouragement, breakdown in faith and practice, and the defeat suffered by God's people, we may be prone to wonder how God will ever realize His family, how the Spirit will finish

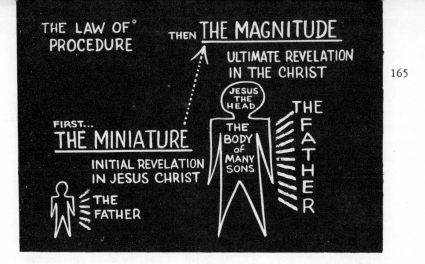

THE LAW OF° PROCEDURE — THEN **THE MAGNITUDE**
ULTIMATE REVELATION IN THE CHRIST

JESUS THE HEAD

THE FATHER

FIRST... **THE MINIATURE**
INITIAL REVELATION IN JESUS CHRIST

THE BODY of MANY SONS

THE FATHER

His temple, and how the Son will ever become the Head over His Body. But we must remember to turn away from this viewpoint *in time*. From the eternal viewpoint God's lovely poem is already complete. As we learn to live in the eternal with Him, we shall see how the future becomes *reality now*.

So we do not look ahead to discover our goal, we look back — back into the Father-heart where it all began. God accomplished His purpose in Christ before the foundation of the world, and we must learn to advance with Him toward the goal on this basis. Spiritual reality has an outstanding characteristic; it bears no marks of time. The time factor vanishes the instant you move into God's viewpoint. In Christian experience then, we move from the beginning on the basis of what already *is* in His eternal outlook. Then as we move into the light of eternal reality, we witness its progressive manifestation. We see every part as it relates to the whole of spiritual realization. ''For the ultimate reality is always before God, and God speaks of His Church in the light of that reality. The time-factor in the Bible is one of the greatest problems to the human mind, but it vanishes from the horizon when once our hearts have been enlightened to know the glory of His inheritance in the saints.'' (Watchman Nee.)

This then is our call: let us not only live *for* the ultimate, but let us live *in the ultimate*. Then life's purpose is not a goal set before us in the future; it is a present, living, reality in which we participate now, even as God does.

IN THE AGES TO COME

All divine intentions have finally crystalized into THE ULTIMATE INTENTION: a family, a body, and a temple—that God might be all and in all. Now, let us see the important place the present dispensation holds as the time in which this masterpiece of God has been taking shape. All past ages waited for and led up to this age. All ages to come take their character from and are governed by what God is doing now.

What about future ages? Some think it entirely inappropriate even to consider such a theme as the "ages to come." Yet the Bible surely draws forth our interest by such references as,

". . . not only in this age but in the ages to come" (Eph. 1:21).

". . . in the ages to come He might shew the exceeding riches of His grace in His kindness toward us through Christ Jesus" (Eph. 2:7).

While we are emphatic at this point to say we have no clear revelation of the ages yet to come, we do know that God has promised them. There is a sense in which we feel as Israel must have felt, when from her Old Testament vantage point she could only see dimly through the shadows what was to transpire in the age beyond the Cross. From our present understanding we are able to see how that age gave character to the age in which we live, even as this age is a dim shadow of what we might expect in the age when Christ shall reign. So the Church, while privileged to have much light, still looks through a glass darkly as regards the future, and waits for that hour when His light and knowledge shall cover the earth as waters cover the sea.

Let us never limit God. Surely there must be some, like Abraham, who have been permitted to look beyond their day to see the city, whose Builder and Maker is God; or like Ezekiel, permitted to behold the temple with the river of life; or like John, have been granted a grandstand seat from which to view "the day of the Lord." And yet we cannot insist that we be permitted individually to look into the ages ahead. We must then be content to study and to understand as the Spirit sheds light on that which God's written Word tells us of the future.

If our eyes have been opened to comprehend even the small portion of GOD'S ULTIMATE INTENTION presented here, 'we have glimpsed enough to thrill our hearts and stir within us a purpose to live with such dedication and devotion as we have not known before. Even so, let it be, Lord Jesus.

WHAT AN UNVEILING IT HAS BEEN to see how these things proceed from the Father-heart, move through time and finally, in consummation, return unto Him. Now in this conclusion we must be sure we have kept our perspective, and that all parts have been properly related to the whole. Momentarily it may have seemed as though the spotlight has been focused too briefly on some phases, yet we have tried to keep every part in its place of relative importance as we see how . . .

The Divine Intention is Realized

A YOUNG LADY had just finished playing a most beautiful series of Chopin nocturnes. "How I love them," she said, "How expressive! They start with a brilliant melody and then suddenly slip into the minor key in which they move along until once again they reach the major key and triumphantly finish with great crescendo and splendor. It seems they picture the whole course of human history! God started with a wonderful purpose, but then Adam sinned and the whole universe turned to a somber theme as if waiting for the hands of the Master Organist to touch the keys and bring forth a brilliant conclusion in the major key. And I think that is what God is doing, but we have been so enveloped in the undertones that our ears have hardly been sensitive to the swelling, increasing crescendo which will soon break forth upon us."

How aptly this friend expressed what we have been trying to demonstrate in this series of lessons. We have written with one deep longing and burden: that somehow we might lift men and their conceptions from the minor key and the consequent undertones, to hear and recognize God's major melody.

It takes little sensitivity of ear to recognize that most of the Church lives in the minor. Too much testimony and preaching reckons from the Fall and emphasizes man's need for recovery, with little or no reference to God's glorious program of ultimate realization. We have discovered how imperative it is to have a proper starting point if we are to keep all things in a proper framework of reference.

GOD – ALL AND IN ALL

It is now possible to recognize what the triune God—Father, Son and Holy Spirit—will each come to realize in ONE ULTIMATE INTENTION.

THE FATHER realizes that which His heart has yearned for throughout the ages: a vast family of sons conformed to the image of His only Begotten—a family who will bring to Him paternal honor, glory and satisfaction.

THE LORD JESUS, as THE SON, receives what the Father has purposed for Him—a many-membered Body which will be for the expression of Himself throughout the universe.

THE HOLY SPIRIT receives a glorious temple built of living stones which will be for His eternal habitation.

Truly so uniquely divine as to be utterly beyond human comprehension, the Godhead—three in One—find individual delight in one great intention: the family, the body, and the temple are one and the same. Both are three in one.

And furthermore, the Father has intended for His Son to have the pre-eminence in all things. It is no marvel then, that the Lord Jesus is referred to as:

The First-born – in the family.

"...*He is the Beginning, the First-born from among the dead, so that He alone in everything and in every respect might occupy the chief place — stand first and be pre-eminent*" (Col. 1:18 A.N.T.).

The Head – of the body.

"...*He also is the Head of (His) body, the church... For it has pleased (the Father) that all the divine fullness—the sum total of the divine perfection, powers and attributes—should dwell in Him permanently*" (Col. 1:18, 19 A.N.T.).

The Chief Cornerstone of the temple.

"... *Behold, I lay in Zion a chosen, precious chief Cornerstone....The very Stone which the builders rejected has become the main Cor-*

ULTIMATE Realization: That God May be All in All

THE FATHER receives A vast family of Sons like the First Born.

THE SON receives A glorious Body for His Expression.

THE HOLY SPIRIT receives a temple of living stones for His Eternal Abode.

THE FIRST BORN THE HEAD CHIEF CORNERSTONE

THE FAMILY BODY TEMPLE

THE THREE IN ONE RECEIVING HONOR GLORY SATISFACTION

nerstone..." (1 Peter 2:6, 7 A.N.T.).

We see then, in all three: whether the family, the body or the temple, the Lord Jesus has the place of pre-eminence. Perhaps this would seem in itself to be a completely satisfying goal. But God's glorious vessel and instrument is only the means to the ultimate goal of which we read in 1 Corinthians 15:28: THAT GOD MIGHT BE ALL AND IN ALL. This is the ultimate realization: the Father, Son, and Spirit will have glory, honor and satisfaction world without end.

It is no wonder that Paul, who had surely glimpsed some of these things, prayed that the Colossians would be able to "see things from His point of view," and would be filled with His wisdom (philosophy); that is, with comprehensive insight into the ways and purpose of God, and with understanding and discernment of spiritual things. (See Colossians 1:9, J. B. Phillips.)

OUR THREE-FOLD THEME

I am sure there are those readers who have glimpsed the fresh beauty and challenge of the Spirit. Let us all remember, we are only in the foothills of the truth the Spirit would reveal. There is always much more in the Word. Here we have spoken of ultimates, yes; but in no sense have we any *full* comprehension of His "ultimate." The finite could never grasp the infinite. Yet, to have glimpsed and experienced even a small measure of the deep rhythm of life in reality on any level enables us to press steadily upward and forward to the divine intention.

There is only one gateway to truth. It is imperative, before we can know any ultimate revelation or realization of His purpose, that we experience the message of the inwrought Cross. By the Cross, God has accomplished an ultimate rectification. Now He invites us to share in its power and its working. When we do, it will make possible our approach to the ultimate revelation wherein every minute fragment of truth fits into its place within the beauty of the whole. What is more! The vision will grip us and carry us along until we see the divine intention ULTIMATELY REALIZED—when every earthly miniature explodes into full heavenly magnitude.

Has the reader a heart-cry for such a vision? God will let us stop with nothing short. True healing for the yearning heart comes when the center of life is outside of self, provided that center is God Himself. May I submit testimonies of some who have entered into God-centered living, not in theory only, but in practice:

"I feel as though I have had a divine shock-treatment which has broken up my old pattern of living and thinking. I've been shocked into re-thinking my philosophy of life, and now relate all to Him."

"For years I was rightly afraid of the philosophy of this world, but now I've found the Person who has become a living philosophy within me."

"At last I've discovered that which I have long sought. I see that Christianity has the ultimate touchstone for a proper starting point. It provides an ultimate goal and the power to move toward that goal."

"For more than 30 years I have preached what I considered a full gospel, but I had never had my own captivity turned. Therefore, I could never bring others to see their greatest need: a rectification in their philosophy of life."

"Although partaking fully of all the intellectual, spiritual, and emotional blessings of fellowship in what is considered a warmly evangelical church group, I suddenly discovered the world was not at all what I thought it to be. In some vague way my church had always revolved around me, and the whole wide world revolved around my church. *Of course I was serving the Lord in this strange world.* But a new vision has gripped me. False worlds revolving around self will pass away, and even the worlds revolving around the church will tumble. Only the great family held together by God's love will remain. This is a family that requires no security but God and has no hope apart from His eternal kingdom."

Voices of men and women who have found Him their all and all testify that He alone is worthy.

FINALLY, to sum up the message of this book and to make a personal application, let us consider a yardstick by which to measure our dedication — whether it is truly an . . .

Ultimate Dedication

EACH INDIVIDUAL lives, moves and plans within a certain framework of reference. The view a person has of the world, of life and of eternity is much like a window which either limits or enhances. Accordingly, all basic concepts of truth are circumscribed by this window or as we shall call it: a framework of reference. "Where there is no vision the people perish," and where there is only a narrow framework of reference there is great limitation! Just as it is impossible for one to live beyond his vision, so it is impossible for one to dedicate beyond his highest goal.

One can hardly appreciate another's viewpoint until he sits where the other sits and appreciates what he sees from his particular framework. This is what Ezekiel meant when he said: " . . . and I sat where they sat . . . " (3:15).

A recent experience brought me to a clearer understanding of this problem. I was visiting with a leader of the Mormon Church. Of course, he assumed that I saw things in the typical framework of most other fundamental believers he had encountered. Assuming my primary interest was "being saved and getting to heaven," he pointed out how short and self-centered this goal seemed to him. Indeed, he was amazed when he discovered that I did not live nor approach truth in that typical framework of "just what God has done and will do for man."

Then he sought to fit me into a bit larger framework of reference. He assumed I must then be primarily interested in the establishment of God's universal kingdom of righteousness on this earth, or the restoration to the Garden of Eden and all that was lost by Adam. His amazement only increased when I assured him that my goal was much larger than that. Then he was sure I must be in accord with his identical framework. So he proceeded to explain how the Mormons had the answer to God's glorious purpose in creating this vast universe. What was the reason? To fill the universe with tested, dedicated human beings who will then enjoy forever all the glory and benefits that God has planned for Himself and His creation. Surely this was far beyond the framework of the average individual. It was his largest framework. Beyond this he could not go, and he was puzzled when I insisted he had not yet really answered God's purpose or ultimate intention. Why did He plan the kingdom? When Adam fell into sin — why did God incorporate redemption?

Now it was my turn, and I assured him that God has revealed in His word the ultimate framework of all reference. While as human beings we cannot know all the vast details of God's ultimate intention, I explained my conviction that God has given this unveiling and it was most necessary to bring each one of us to supreme or ultimate dedication to it. Then I proceeded to draw for him this simple diagram showing the three most common frameworks of reference and then introducing the necessity of the Ultimate Framework:

FRAMEWORK 1. For those who are primarily occupied with personal salvation, their framework begins with man's fall into sin and ends with man's redemption and getting to heaven. But since it starts with man, it ends with man and what he gets. We must not discount this part, but we must see it properly related to a larger framework of truth.

FRAMEWORK 2. Others seem almost to by-pass any need for personal redemption. They almost ignore the Fall and become involved in the establishing of God's kingdom purposes. Just talk with anyone who is really indoctrinated in the national message — a Jehovah's Witness or a devotee of British-Israel teaching — and you find how their framework is concerned with God's kingdom and His righteous government on the earth. This framework determines their dedication which is "bringing in the kingdom." Alas, there are many liberals — and many cultists who start with Adam as king in the garden and end with man as universal king on the earth.

FRAMEWORK 3. Then there are those who start with the Eternal

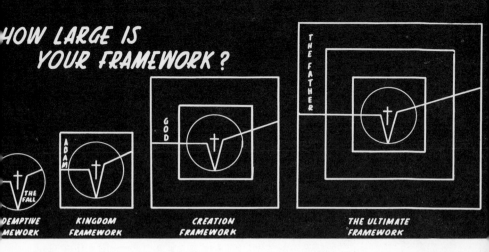

HOW LARGE IS YOUR FRAMEWORK?

DEMPTIVE | KINGDOM | CREATION | THE ULTIMATE
MEWORK | FRAMEWORK | FRAMEWORK | FRAMEWORK

God as Creator. Beginning with God in His Genesis creation, they seek to find meaning and reason for this vast creation. There are numerous interpretations, but for even the most devoted fundamentalist, this framework seems to stop with man conformed to the image of God and finally enjoying all that God intended in a "new creation."

The whole creation is on tiptoe to see the wonderful sight of the sons of God coming into their own. The world of creation cannot as yet see Reality, not because it chooses to be blind, but because in God's purpose it has been so limited—yet it has been given hope. And the hope is that IN THE END the whole of created life will be rescued from the tyranny of change and decay, and have its share in that magnificent liberty which can only belong to the children of God!

It is plain to anyone with eyes to see that at the present time all created life groans in a sort of universal travail (Rom. 8:19-22 J. B. Phillips).

So all creation will be delivered! He has said it: "Behold, I make all things new" (Rev. 21:5). But there must be some greater reason. New! For what?

Although the dedication in this third framework is that God might (in this hour when "ALL THINGS ARE NEW") have the glory and honor and in a sense this goes beyond what man is to get, yet this view is still too small. There is a larger and more ultimate framework which gives ultimate meaning.

FRAMEWORK 4. Finally we come to the ULTIMATE FRAMEWORK of REFERENCE. If we have not realized it, we shall be surprised that it starts way back in the Father-heart — not merely *with the foundation* but *before* the foundation of the world. As we have pointed out, Paul by very special revelation starts in Ephesians with "The God and Father of our Lord Jesus" who is the First Cause of all causes. It was not man's Fall that determined all things; it was not God's desire for a kingdom, nor even His plan for a new creation—but it was God's paternal being and nature which determined His primary desire, His eternal purpose, His supreme dedication and finally the ultimate realization which will bring to Him that satisfaction of which His Father-heart is so worthy.

What framework could be larger than the one beginning with the eternal Father and ending with that vast family which will bring to Him and His eternal Son honor, glory, pleasure and satisfaction? In such a framework we see the importance of salvation (since man did fall). We see the kingdom; we see the New Creation, but we also see the Father and His vast family. This gives proper meaning to all that is included.

Turn again to Paul's words in Romans 8 and see if they have more meaning:

And it is plain, too . . . that at last we have realized our full sonship in Him.

Moreover we know that to those who love God, who are called according to His Plan, everything that happens fits into a pattern for good. God, in his foreknowledge, chose them to bear the family likeness of His Son, that He might be the elder of a family of many brothers. He chose them long ago; when the time came He called them, He made them righteous in His sight and then lifted them to the splendour of life as His own sons (Rom. 8:28-30 J. B. Phillips).

Living in the glory of all that He shall some day realize in us causes us to forget not only all our present suffering, but also our own private goals and ambitions. Every cause that once seemed so important and imperative now becomes adjusted to the ULTIMATE INTENTION.

THEN WHAT IS OUR DEDICATION? We see how it is the truth that sets us free from every lesser dedication. Now that we have moved into the eternal stream where we see all from His own viewpoint—now, our dedication could be nothing less than helping Him to realize His glorious plan and ULTIMATE INTENTION.

Now to Him who is able to keep you from stumbling, and cause you to stand in the presence of His glory free from blemish and exultant—to the only God our Saviour through Jesus Christ our Lord—be glory, majesty, might, and authority, before all time, now and to all time! Amen. (Jude 24-25, Weymouth).

This Important Distinction

IN SHARING ULTIMATE TRUTH with others, the reader will probably encounter two extreme attitudes. There are those who have so long allowed the immediate and present needs to overshadow, that they can hardly see any value or have any true appreciation for anything long-range or ultimate. They will insist on being more practical and realistic.

But there are others who will follow another extreme. Some who have merely an intellectual fancy for truth will reach for this (as they do other things) and make it a present hobby. This type of mind will ignore any practical, immediate or present need and dwell only on the ultimate. For them, it is just another way of escaping responsibility, repentance or reality. Many sincere people have been "innoculated against the truth" by observing those who hold it intellectually but have never allowed it to become operative in their life as reality.

So there is a difference between "knowing about the ultimate" and "living in the ultimate." The first is only intellectual. However one who is truly "living in the ultimate" cannot help but see every *immediate need* as it relates to the whole *ultimate scope*. What appears to be a hundred separate and unrelated needs or crises then are actually but different phases of a single whole. In God's viewpoint everything is related to everything else—as it relates to Him. The Holy Spirit will help us to be alert and sensitive to every immediate need while we continue to hold the eternal and ultimate clearly before us. In ourselves we are prone to imbalance. Only in God do we find the balance of the immediate and the ultimate.

It has been our thesis from the beginning that men are prone to overlook the long-range or ultimate, and like Esau of old, become nearsighted in living only for the immediate. We have been seeking to keep every immediate issue in alignment with the ultimate goal: this is walking in HIS perception and perspective.

One day I sat in a pastor's study as a member of his congregation approached. Every week for more than a year this lady had come with a new crisis which needed an immediate cure. That morning however, we were able to press back beyond her immediate needs and I'm sure, the Lord helped this dear mother and wife to see the wrong course of the whole background and pattern of her life during the past twenty years. She saw how the present was simply the harvest of long years of wrong planting. Thus fruit would be inevitable and continue until God got at the root of the trouble. She saw it was not God's way to live in the state of emergency in daily pruning the branches; God wanted to destroy the tree and plant another, this would mean a new conception of life. It was so drastic! But the Holy Spirit always is. He wanted her to see the difference between mere *crisis-living* and a *long-range course.*

May God help every one of us as His servants to carry the immediate cure in our hearts, but even more, to live with our eyes open to God's preventative approach: Jesus Christ must become in every life the power for *living by pattern* and *living by principle.*

REMEMBER! We begin to look like that which our eyes steadily gaze upon. Our thoughts, ambitions, dedication and motives are the architects which mold us into their image. Having molded our inner man, they even shape our physical appearance. The fertilizing element contained in these ultimate thoughts is pointed out by the poet who said:

> Whenever you cultivate a thought,
> Remember it will trace
> With certain touch in pictured form
> A story on your face.

> Whenever you dwell upon a thought,
> Remember it will roll
> Into your being and become
> A fiber of your soul.

> Whenever you send out a thought,
> Remember it will be
> A force throughout the universe
> For all eternity.

Acknowledgements

IN HARMONY WITH THE MESSAGE and emphasis of this book, it seems more appropriate to call this "our book" instead of "my book." Perhaps this is even more true than we realize of most of what is written. As we rapidly approach the hour when God must mature the Church, His Body, it seems that only a "body-ministry" can meet the real needs of His Body. Therefore we rejoice in the total contribution of many who have helped either directly or indirectly in the preparation and production of this volume. While there have been many hidden behind the scenes working as a labor of love, there are these to whom we are specially indebted:

To C. ARNELL JONES of Van Wert, Ohio, who for more than twenty years has shared spiritual inspiration, patient teaching and wise counseling which have put an indelible imprint on this writing. From his writings and teaching have come many of the seeds of truth which we have clothed in our own expression. We have used several quotations from his manuscript: *The Supreme and Final Thing*. So familiar have we become with his writings, and the writings of several others who are spearheading a revolt against this present-day humanism, that we find ourselves quoting them almost verbatim. Indulgence is begged, therefore, if there has been any failure of proper acknowledgment, or if we have failed to reach the author or holder of copywrited selections.

To Miss RUTH NOURSE of Mt. Vernon, Mo., for valuable help in the evaluating and rewriting of the manuscript.

To my sweet wife, NITA, who has almost lived at the typewriter for days in the preparation of this volume and the issues of the Journal.

To JAMES SEWARD of Cleveland, Ohio, for his labor of love in preparing the many blackboard drawings.

To LORENE FIEKER and DEAN BAKER of Mt. Vernon, Mo., for their proof-reading.

To the CHRISTENSON FAMILY of Cowiche, Washington, whose giving to SURE FOUNDATION has made possible the printing of this volume.

To the MANY FRIENDS who have faithfully prayed that God might through the printed page awaken His children to God-centered living.

We also acknowledge the great kindness of various authors and publishers, who have granted permission to use quotations from their copywrited publications:

To CHRISTIAN PUBLICATIONS for selections from editorials in *The Alliance Witness* and in *Born After Midnight* by A. W. Tozer.

To CHRISTIAN SCHOOLS SERVICE for quotation from *Christian Philosophy*, Vol. 1 by Mark Fakkema.

To CHANNEL PRESS, INC. for quotation in *Victory over Suffering* by A. Graham Ikin.

To BETHANY FELLOWSHIP PRESS for quotation from *Three Aspects of the Cross* by T. A. Hegre.

To CHRISTIAN LITERATURE CRUSADE for quotations from *The Normal Christian Life* and *What Shall This Man Do* by Watchman Nee, and *The Liberating Secret* by Norman Grubb.

To WITNESS AND TESTIMONY PUBLISHERS for quotations from writings of T. Austin Sparks.

To CHRISTIANITY TODAY for quotations.

To WM. B. EERDMANS PUBLISHING CO. for quotations from *Ephesians and Colossians in the Greek New Testament* by Kenneth S. Wuest.

To ZONDERVAN PUBLISHING HOUSE for use of quotations from *The Amplified New Testament*.

To HARPER AND BROTHERS for quotation from Fulton J. Sheen in *Best Sermons* of 1946.

To THE OVERCOMER for quotations by Mrs. Penn-Lewis in *Memoirs*, and other quotations from R. B. Jones.

Appendix

IT HAS SEEMED advisable in this new, enlarged edition to place some of the appendix material at the rear of the book so as to assure better continuity of the main theme and also that the reader might not be discouraged with heavy details or addendum subjects.

Those who have been using this book as a guide for midweek study or in Bible school courses will find this additional material helpful. In this first year alone, we have been thrilled and amazed to learn that eighty pastors and teachers (and we believe many more we do not know of) have been using this as a guide for their class or group. We rejoice! But we also pray that those who use this book may be sure to present quickened truth as the Holy Spirit has made it personally alive in them, not merely as a manual for sharing more knowledge.

Further, we have appreciated the fine response from pastors, Bible teachers and professors in schools. Many have suggested these valuable clarifications for our new edition and we include them here in the appendix with the reminder to our readers once again: "Surely this has been a corporate production and a body-ministry directed by the Spirit to His Church-at-large."

Added material for
Chapter One

WHAT IS CHRISTIAN PHILOSOPHY?

BECAUSE there is so much false philosophy in our day, it is extremely important that God's children understand the important place of the true divine philosophy. Many have misunderstood Paul's statement in Colossians 2:8: "Beware lest any man spoil you through philosophy and vain deceit, after the tradition of men, after the rudiments of the world, and not after Christ."

Note that he is warning against the false philosophy "after the tradition of men''—but there is a true philosophy which is ''after Christ.''

Our safety is in becoming occupied with Christ. He then becomes our philosophy just as automatically as the driver at the steering wheel of the car becomes its director and determiner.

Dr. Mark Fakkema, in his *Vol. 1 of Christian Philosophy*, shows the imperative necessity of seeing God as THE ULTIMATE and how this determines a truly Christian philosophy.

"Christian philosophy is the romance of seeing all things whole with God as ultimate." This definition of philosophy comprises three elements:

(a) PHILOSOPHY IS A ROMANCE. A romance culminating in marriage is two individuals becoming one. Every true marriage is the union of two persons (Gen. 2:24; Mark 10:7-9). Philosophy is the romance of all romances. It intellectually unites all things in one pattern of thought.

(b) WE MUST SEE ALL THINGS WHOLE. Philosophy is seeing unity amid variety. From Thales to John Dewey, philosophers have endeavored to integrate all things.

(c) GOD IS THE ULTIMATE. To see all things whole, calls for a point of ''reference'' which is a point of ''coordination'' that unites all into one pattern of thought. The point that coordinates all this is the Ultimate. It can also be described as Primary Reality (creation is secondary reality) or as the First Cause beyond which we cannot go. God is the ULTIMATE for Christian philosophy.

''Philosophy is therefore not a collection of the totality of things. It is an integration of all things brought about by an interpretation of all things as dependent or derivative of something or someone. This something or someone we call God, the ULTIMATE of all things. (It is also referred to as the point of reference or of coordination.) In Christian philosophy this Ultimate is God—the God of the Bible. We can illustrate the meaning of Ultimate thus:

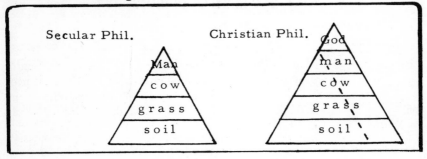

"If the universe consisted of only two things, namely, soil and grass, then grass would be the Ultimate, for the soil may be said to exist for the grass. That is to say, the soil yields its ingredients to the grass as a matter of course. If the universe were confined to three things, soil, grass and a cow, then the cow would obviously be the Ultimate. If the universe consisted of soil, grass, cow and a man, then man would be the Ultimate.

"But man is not the Ultimate of our universe. As the soil yields to the grass, as the grass yields to the cow, and as the cow yields to man, so man in turn must surrender himself to God. Whereas non-Christian philosophies would subject God to what they consider to be Ultimate, Christian philosophy subjects all things—including ourselves —to God as ULTIMATE. It is evident that such a philosophy by implication makes for humility and yieldedness on our part."

Added material for
Chapter Two:

THOSE WHO CONFIRM: WE MUST START
WITH THE FATHER AS THE TOUCHSTONE

It would seem there are many voices today insisting that we must not overlook THE FATHER as our touchstone and starting point for all true and final reckoning. This does not infer, however, that we can come to the Father in any other way except through the Son, the Lord Jesus Christ. Truly He is the only door and the only way unto the Father. In this sense Christ Jesus is always our starting point so far as personal redemption is concerned, but as we have indicated in chapter two, the Father is the proper starting point for understanding all ultimate revelation, rectification and realization.

It seems also to be the conviction of P. B. Fitzwater, former professor of Systematic Theology of Moody Bible Institute, that men have often emphasized the part of "saviourhood" but have missed ·the importance of Fatherhood as it determines the whole:

"Careful thought and observation reveal a surpassing lack of reference to God as Father in the speech and prayers of Christians today, while there is constant reference to Jesus Christ as the Saviour. Saviourhood is much emphasized while the Fatherhood of God is given comparatively little attention. Few of our hymns are addressed to God or even describe Him as to His essential character and grace. It is sometimes painfully embarrassing to be unable to find a hymn setting forth the Fatherhood of God. There is one Triune God. Our thought, therefore, should be balanced by giving the proper recognition to the Persons of the Godhead. The New Testament persistently sets forth God the Father as the primary source and ultimate goal of the believer's life. God the Father was persistently in the thought and on the lips of Jesus Christ. In the New Testament, Father is the predominant title used by the Lord Jesus Christ to express His personal relation to God. The well-instructed Christian will not fail to note Christ's emphasis on God as His own Father, and the Father of all believers.''

This concept of God's Fatherhood has also been strikingly expressed by Dr. James Orr in his *Sidelights on Christian Doctrine*, and is as follows:

"The Fatherhood of God in the full Christian idea of it does not originate with God's relation to the world or to man or heaven with God's relation to believers. God was a Father before He had relation either to the world or to believers. He is Father in Himself, the Father everlasting. This again implies the triune concept. If you wish to find the ultimate spring of Fatherhood in the heart of God, you must seek it not in relation to humanity or to believers, but in the relation to the eternal and only begotten Son. (John 1:18). It is with this Fatherly love of which the primal object is the Son that God turns to the world and seeks to draw men in to be sharers of it.''

Again let us consider the words of A. Graham Ikin who pleads that we must see all parts in their proper framework of reference: "We have made too much of the suffering of Christ on the Cross, not because it was not real enough (it may even have been far greater than our narrow minds can conceive) but because it was a remedial activity within the framework of the wider creativity of the Father-Godhead which was primary." *(In Victory Over Suffering.)*

Added material for
Chapter Three:

DID GOD CREATE SIMPLY IN ORDER TO REDEEM?

As we go to press with this second edition we have just read James I. Packers' review of a new book, CHURCH DOGMATICS by Karl Barth, in which he evaluates this problem of whether Christ is related to things or whether things are related to Christ:

"The chief problems with which the book confronts us spring directly from Barth's conception of the Christocentricity of Scripture. It is methodologically unbiblical, Barth holds, to interpret the fact of Christ in terms of the doctrine of creation and the fall; rather, the relation must be reversed and creation itself interpreted in terms of God's purpose in Christ. This inverting of the method followed by all Protestant dogmatics hitherto leads to some controversial pieces of exposition. Thus, the New Testament teaching that all things were made in and through the Son is held to mean not that the Word was active as Creator when the world began but that when God created he had in view, and was prompted by, his already formed purpose to glorify Jesus Christ as the incarnate Mediator."

Inasmuch as we have not read this work of Barth we cannot judge whether the reviewer has correctly interpreted him. However, lest anyone should mistakenly make the same judgment from our writings, let it be said that God's glorious work of realization was to be accomplished through Jesus Christ and when the work of rectification became necessary, then He, too, was the means by which that should be effected. But the reviewer continues:

"Similarly, the statement that God approved what he had made as 'very good' has, according to Barth, nothing to do with an original excellence now marred by sin, but due to be restored through Christ; all it means is that the created order, such as it was, was perfectly adapted for the fulfillment of the plan of grace. The 'goodness' of creation is thus as much a fact now as ever it was; indeed, it is precisely because God has thus approved it as a means to this end that this present world must be judged the best possible. In all this Barth seems to be saying *that God created simply in order to redeem;* which supralapsarianism, thus expressed, would seem to rob the fall of its biblical significance."

It is this very snare in our thinking—that God must have created in order to redeem — that we have been exposing in this treatise.

Added material for
Chapter Four:

AN INVITATION TO JOIN THE "ETERNAL KOINONIA"

It is true in all our relationships among men that we can only fellowship or participate with others according to our knowledge or experience. For this reason God is progressively leading us into fuller knowledge and deeper experience. It is in order that we might come to the fullest understanding of Himself and His desire, purpose and intention. The more we approach this measure of the Divine wisdom and understanding the more we can see the parts related to the whole. Then we can live in that ultimate fellowship which the Father, Son and Holy Spirit have enjoyed from the beginning. And we can better understand:

What did God do before the foundation of the world? This question has received very different answers. Some have simply declared it to be unjustified (Luther); others have attempted to explain it philosophically (Origen). The Bible takes a middle course, in that it at the same time conceals and reveals, and with divine condescension clothes its information as to the eternal and super-temporal matters in the form of thoughts from the realm of creation and space (e.g. Isa. 43:10).

"For God Himself as the eternal there is no limit of time, no sequence of before and after. He surveys all times at once, and therefore to Him the world in all its extensions is already eternally present.

"Before the foundation of the whole universe God had been in eternal loving intercourse with His Son. Thus in the beginning, this Word was already with God, present eternally with Him in the intercourse of a mutually responsive fellowship. And the Father loved the Son, who afterwards testified on earth, 'Thou lovedst me before the foundation of the world' (John 17:24). 'And now glorify thou me, Father, with thyself, with the glory which I possessed with thee before the world was' (John 17:5). (Erich Sauer in *The Dawn of World Redemption.*)

"It is exciting to realize that God did not exist in solitary aloneness from eternity, prior to the creation of the world and man, but in a blessed communion.

"Although Jesus Christ is the proper magnetic center of our faith, and although faith in Him distinguishes ours from other religions such as Judaism and Unitarianism, we evangelical Protestants are sometimes prone to relegate the Father and the Holy Spirit to lesser importance. It is to be expected that we would feel close to the One who 'pitched His tent' among us; who bit dust for us, wept for us, died for us, is coming to translate us. Stressing the deity of Christ as we need to do, we might tend to make the begotten One the first instead of the second person of the Trinity. The three are of equal dignity, majesty, glory, power, eternity. Each has all the divine attributes. But the Father has a priority in eternally generating the Son, and the Holy Spirit proceeds from the Father and the Son. The fact that the incarnate Son obeys the Father, along with the Biblical protrayal of the Holy Spirit as peculiarly characterized by personal self-effacement, also points to the priority of the Father. Whereas Jesus said that He and the Father are one (John 10:30). He also said, 'My Father is greater than I' (John 14:28). He declared, 'For I have not spoken of myself; but the Father which sent me, He gave me a commandment, what I should say, and what I should speak' (John 12:49). (In *Christianity Today* — J. Kenneth Grider, professor of Systematic Theology, Theological Seminary, Kansas City, Missouri.)

Added material for
Chapter Five:

THIS IS WHAT HAPPENS IN LIVING FROM A NEW CENTER

"The secret of happiness is centeredness. The God-responsive soul becomes deaf to the promptings of the senses, for to him *God is everything*. Like great cosmic dynamos these souls generate energy by which other souls on the circumference can live. Life for God-responsive souls now begins to move from a circumference to a center. The externals of life, such as politics, economics and its daily routine, matter less, while God matters more. This does not mean that humanity is unloved, but that it is loved more in God. The now-moment becomes a servant to the Eternal-moment. The uninteresting, the unreal is now what is not used or cannot be used for God's purpose. There is no dart in the quiver of a Godly soul for anything but the Divine-Target.

"The God-responsive soul thinks of religion in terms of submission to the will of God. He does not look to the Infinite to help him in his finite interests but, rather, seeks to surrender his finite interests to the Infinite. His prayer is 'Not my will, but Thine, be done, O Lord.' No longer interested in using God, he wants God to use him. Like Mary, he says, 'Be it done unto Me according to Thy Word,' or like Paul he asks, 'What wilt Thou have me to do, O Lord?' or like John the Baptist he says, 'I must decrease, he must increase.'

"The destruction of egotism and selfishness so that the whole mind may thus be subject to the Divine Personality does not entail a disinterest in the active life; it brings a greater interest, because the man now understands life from God's point of view. Because of his unity with the Divine Source of energy, he has greater power to do good—as a soldier is stronger under a great general than a poor one. 'If you abide in me, and my words abide in you, you shall ask whatever you will and it shall be done unto you. In this is my Father glorified; that you bring forth very much fruit' (John 15:7-8). It is hard for self-centered creatures to realize that there are some souls that are really and truly passionately in love with God. But this should not be so hard to understand; he who loves the light and heat of the candle should surely love the sun-light even more."   (From *Peace of Soul* by F. J. Sheen.)

Added material for
Chapter Six:

THE REVOLT IS SPREADING

WHILE WE SEEM ALMOST overwhelmed by the utter blindness of the present evangelical leadership, we rejoice that God has a few voices who dare to cry out against the humanistic trend and man-centered emphasis apparent on every hand:

"Some moderns are determined to dress up Christ in a grey flannel suit, to make Him blend perfectly into the contemporary picture. The attempt is an obvious travesty of the Christ of the Scriptures.

"The Gospel today, in some quarters, is so smothered in adjustment opinions that it is scarcely recognizable. It is really a new religion. Some of the familiar words and names are there, but the aims, the methods, and the message have been grounded. They are earthly, man-centered, horizontally oriented. This religion is typified by a sign I saw on a large church in St. Louis: 'The church is your first business, because if the church fails, America's business fails.' It is easy to see that the ultimate in this faith is in reality secular. It is of man, by man and for man; God is relevant only insofar as He is an aid to man's progress and well-being." (Robert H. Lawer in *Christianity Today.*)

"Nothing has been or can be more detrimental to man and to his greatest good and glory than to believe that Bible evangelism or gospel preaching is primarily for his own personal benefit, security, enjoyment and satisfaction. For the One who created man for His glory and pleasure is the same One who is now saving him for the very same purpose.

"Evangelism that is chiefly motivated by man's lost and unhappy condition, his untold worth and potentialities, his awful need and imminent danger, and the great benefits that will accrue to him by being saved is not Bible or Christian evangelism but humanism. Christian evangelism does comprehend all that man is, needs and will enjoy by being saved, but this is not the major concern and end of Christian evangelism. For the thing that man has been lost from through sin, and is now being saved from, to and for is the thing of primary importance. There is an evangelism that is primarily devoted to the revelation and realization of that which God Himself chiefly is, desires, wills and intends. And this is evangelism on its highest plain, in its greatest role, seeking its greatest ultimate." (From C. A. Jones in *The Supreme and Final Thing.*)

"The flaw in current evangelism lies in its humanistic approach. It struggles to be supernaturalistic but never quite makes it. It is frankly fascinated by the great, noisy, aggressive world with its big name, its hero worship, its wealth and its garish pageantry. To the millions of disappointed persons who have always yearned for worldly glory but never attained to it, the modern evangel offers a quick and easy shortcut to their heart's desire. Peace of mind, happiness, prosperity, social acceptance, publicity, success in sports, business, the entertainment field, and perchance to sit occasionally at the same banquet table with a celebrity—all this on earth and heaven at last. Certainly no insurance company can offer half as much.

"In this quasi-Christian scheme of things God becomes the Aladdin lamp who does the bidding of everyone that will accept His Son and sign a card. The total obligation of the sinner is discharged when he accepts Christ. After that he has but to come with his basket and receive the religious equivalent of everything the world offers and enjoy it to the limit. Those who have not accepted Christ must be content with this world, but the Christian gets this one with the one to come thrown in as a bonus.

"Such is the Christian message as interpreted by vast numbers of religious leaders today. This gross misapprehension of the truth is back of much (I almost said most) of our present evangelical activity. It determines directions, builds programs, decides the content of sermons, fixes the quality of local churches and even of whole denominations, sets the pattern for religious writers and forms the editorial policy of many evangelical publications.

"This concept of Christianity is in radical error, and because it touches the souls of men it is a dangerous, even deadly, error. At bottom it is little more than weak humanism allied with weak Christianity to give it ecclesiastical respectability. It may be identified by its religious approach. Invariably it begins with man and his needs, and then looks around for God; true Christianity reveals God as searching for man to deliver him from his ambitions." (From *Born After Midnight*, by A. W. Tozer.)

"The prevailing religious mood of the next generation, he predicts will be God-centered rather than man-centered. The bankruptcy of humanism will steadily drive religious thought back to the acknowledgement of God as personally active in the universe" (G. Colman Luck in MOODY MONTHLY reviewing *Science Returns to God*, by James Jaunsey).

Added material for
Chapter Seven:

RECTIFICATION ADDS A LARGER MEANING

SINCE WE HAVE in several places used the translation of Ferrar Fenton, a word of explanation is in order that you might understand our reasons. For a deeper appreciation and understanding of Mr. Fenton's desire in translating the Scriptures let me quote from his own introductory notes:

"In the year 1853 there was inspired into my mind, by what appeared a mere accident, a resolve to study the Bible absolutely in its original languages, to ascertain what its writers actually said and taught. I am now writing in 1903, just fifty years after, and have accomplished my object, and completed an entirely new translation of the whole of the Hebrew and Christian Scriptures direct from the Hebrew, Chaldee, and Greek, in which they were first given to the world.

"I at once threw myself into the stream of the suggestion and registered a vow that I would never again read the Gospels, or Christian Documents of our Faith, in any language but Greek, until I had learned to think in that tongue and it had become as familiar to me as the diction of an English newspaper."

Now however noble the vow and worthwhile the dedication, this fact still remains. Man can never hope, even in a million years of reading the original language, to uncover the divine meaning unless the Holy Spirit quickens and reveals. Fenton, of course, claims he enjoyed this measure of revelation. It awaits our evaluation and the increasing light of these last days to help us determine how right he was.

If the reader asks for my own comment, I would agree with others that very often Fenton takes a liberty in translating certain words and phrases which has quite weakened his work and for this reason, perhaps, his translation is not widely used or even recommended. Our use of just a few verses should in no way be construed as a blanket approval for his whole work. But that is also true of any other translation we use. Many have written asking where they might obtain this translation and who Fenton is. We have generally discouraged their using it.

This question then: Why do we use it at all? Let me answer in the words of G. C. Berkouwer:

"We must remain open for any correction of our thought that the Word may at any time insist upon. Indeed, our preoccupation with the Bible means nothing if it does not mean that we keep ourselves open, open to more and clearer understanding.   If one studies Kittel's theological dictionary of the New Testament—a monumental work now at the threshold of completion—he is more deeply impressed than ever with the limited character of human speech about the Bible. This does not mean that our speech is worthless because it is mere human speech. The Church was and still is called to confess. But it must confess in humility. It must never leave the impression that its speech is final, that the last word about Scripture on any point has now been said. The Church must make it very clear that it stands under the scepter of the Gospel and that it can never be content merely to repeat yesterday's words, the words which the Church used yesterday for confessing the truth."—*Christianity Today*

This is to say that many of the words which we have used in our common language have taken on different, or (really) lost meaning. Therefore, if we can find some word which adds another side or freshness or even a new shade or largeness of meaning—it brings to the mind a new insight. Surely no single word we use can possibly translate all the Spirit intended. It must be revealed—must be an impartation which comes direct. Yet we are forced to use words when we think.

Let us consider three instances in which Fenton's use of another word might bring a new and larger meaning. If we could be free from our somewhat sterile or prejudiced conceptions, we might see how the usage of these words adds new shades of meaning. We do not mean to use these only, but sometimes it takes several words to give full meaning—as the Amplified New Testament has done.

Fenton translates the word "doxa" as *rectification* instead of as *glory* which is commonly accepted in the King James. In some ways this may seem to weaken instead of strengthen the real content. This is true especially if we consider the word "rectify" (to make or set right, to amend) only from man's viewpoint. Then we miss the meaning entirely. Remember we have started in the beginning by showing what rectification means from God's viewpoint; how He longs and desires for man to be wholly aligned and in tune with His great purpose and plan. Only then do we bring glory to God.

To bring man to the place where God receives glory in him requires a moral, spiritual, physical and mental rectification. But it requires even more. Too often we have overlooked man's great need for a philosophical rectifying—a rectifying in his purpose and intention in life. Thus Fenton, in Colossians 1:27, speaks of "the mystery of rectification which Christ is to you—the hope of the rectification—which we proclaim." I believe he is contending that when a thing is truly right unto God, it is glorious—full of glory both to God and toward man.

If we could be sure to see in "doxa" that glory which focuses our mind and heart on God, rather than merely that glory which man will enjoy, we could be content in always using the word *glory* instead of *rectify*. But our hope in using this translation at least, was to show how gray can sharpen white when alongside of it.

Take the word "sophia" which is translated *wisdom* in the King James, but which Fenton translates as philosophy. Some may think this unjustified by contending that the word "philosophia" which means love of wisdom is used as it should be in Colossians 2:8. But I think this is straining at technicality. Throughout the early part of first Corinthians, Paul is dealing with those who, imbibed in philosophical reasoning, were unable to receive the true wisdom or divine philosophy of God. The natural man may forever pry into the mysteries of Greece, yet will forever be shut out from the spiritual things which must be revealed by God. We are convinced that our difficulty is not in the use of this term, but rather in a failure to understand the snare of the worldly philosopher: he has a preoccupation, not with receiving wisdom from God, but rather with the love of searching out wisdom by his own powers so as to inflate his own ego.

Take another word in Colossians 1:26 translated from the Greek "logos" which Fenton translates as the *divine intention* instead of as the "word of God." It would seem that the broader meaning of the word "logos" should include this aspect. Does it not enlarge our thinking to realize that all the mind, will, purpose and intent of God is expressed either in the pages of Holy Writ, the written Word, or in His Son, the Living Word? Thus God's divine intention is expressed in a manifold way.